THE FORGOTTEN FEAR

THE FORGOTTEN FEAR

Are you afraid yet?
You should be!

DR. PAUL T. EVANS

Scripture taken from the New King James Version.
Copyright © 1982 by Thomas Nelson, Inc.
Used by permission. All rights reserved.

Copyright © 2023 Paul T. Evans

All rights reserved. No part of this book may be used or reproduced in any manner whatsoever without written permission of the author. Published 2023.

Printed in the United States of America.

ISBN: 978-1-63385-495-6
Library of Congress Control Number: 2023906847

Published by
Word Association Publishers
205 Fifth Avenue
Tarentum, Pennsylvania 15084

www.wordassociation.com
1.800.827.7903

Contents

Acknowledgements and Dedication..........................vii

Foreword ix

Introduction..xiii

An Important Note xvii

1   The Comprehensive Definition of the Fear of God 1

2   The Levels of the Fear of God 19

3   The Characteristics of Those Who Fear God 27

4   The Benefits and Consequences of Fearing or Not Fearing God........................... 47

5   What Causes Us to Lose the Fear of The Lord?... 89

6   The Complete List of All the Verses in the Bible that Speak to the Fear of God 129

7   The Fear of God Assessment Tool and Evaluation..161

Conclusion 165

About the Author 169

Acknowledgements and Dedication

I WOULD LIKE TO THANK everyone who has helped in the writing and editing of this book. Most of all I want to express my love, devotion, and gratefulness to my wonderful wife, Mandy, who first received this word from the Lord and the many hours through the years that she encouraged me and deeply discussed so much of what is now written in this book. Because of all of this:

I formally dedicate this book to **Mandy Marie Evans.**

My partner in this life,
The love of my life,
And my loving wife in whom I am well pleased!

Foreword

AS YOU SURVEY THE LANDSCAPE of Christianity, there are a host of biblical topics that seem to garner a great deal of attention. We love to talk about the love and grace of God. We love to talk about the promises and power of Jesus. We love to talk about the Second Coming of Christ and, it is for good reason that we study those Biblical themes – God clearly wants us to study them because He clearly taught them in His word, the Bible.

However, there are certain themes of Scripture that are just as clearly taught in the Bible but seem to be avoided by many modern Christians. One of those biblical themes is the fear of God. Almost no one is talking about the fear of God. Many people live out a so-called version of "Christianity" that approaches God casually and treats His holiness lightly, but Hebrews 12:28-29 says that by the grace of God to us in Jesus, "*we may serve*

God acceptably with reverence and godly fear. For our God is a consuming fire." Whether or not our world wants to have the conversation, our Holy God has made it clearly known that He is a consuming fire. We simply cannot serve Him acceptably without reverence and godly fear.

That's why I am grateful for Dr. Paul Evans and his diligent study of this powerful biblical truth. In *The Forgotten Fear,* Dr. Evans has compiled an extensive survey of the Bible's teaching relating to the fear of God. As I read through the pages of this book, there were several things that made me thank God for his approach to this study:

1. I thank God this book is saturated with the Scripture. Who knows better than God what is means for us to live in the fear of God? Dr. Evans has included nearly 200 scriptures that directly teach us what God Himself has to say about living in the fear of God. I encourage you to read this book in the spirit with which Dr. Evans wrote it: as a Bible study and not simply the thoughts of a man.

2. I thank God this book presents a balanced view of the fear of God. Throughout my life and ministry, I have heard teachers emphasize a single dimension of the fear of God. Whether it's the aspect of awe and worship or of fear and trembling, many teachers and authors tend to settle on just one aspect of what the Bible teaches about the fear of God. In my opinion, this usually results in a lopsided view

of God in which God is either so fearful that we are not compelled to intimacy with Him or He is so benign that there is no trembling in His presence. I thank God for Dr. Evans' presentation of the multi-faceted nature of the fear of God. As you read through the "Seven Features," I encourage you to take your time and meditate on each one. Allow the Lord to give you a full view of what it looks like to live in the fear of God.

3. I thank God for the practical insights this book provides on living in the fear of God. This is not merely a theological conversation without practical implications for our lives. Dr. Evans draws on his background of life and ministry to help us consider the way our daily lives should reflect the fear of the Lord. This book is intended to do more than just change your mind; it's aimed at changing your life.

As you read this book, my prayer is that you will find yourself being renewed in a biblical vision of the one, true God. May you encounter our God who is "a consuming fire." May you learn what it means to "serve God acceptably with reverence and godly fear." May you rejoice in the grace of Jesus, who enables and empowers such a life.

Titus Green, *Lead Pastor*
First Baptist Church, Merritt Island, Florida

Introduction

ONCE IN A LIFETIME, a spiritual man would long to receive a special life-changing word from the Lord that would be for all people for all time. This happened to me in 2002. It resulted in authoring a book called "The Forgotten Commandment." The word from the Lord was regarding what it really means to love other people like Jesus loves us and the fact that the Christian Church in general had lost or forgotten what the scriptures actually teach about this matter. It also led to teaching this word to as many people around the world who would listen. To this day, there are hundreds of Grace Christian Fellowship Churches that we have helped to start around the world that are living and walking in that love of God and practicing the particular "One another" verses found in the New Testament. These churches are growing and continuing to reach souls for Christ in vast numbers and new churches are starting almost every month. Yes, villages, cities, and countries are being changed by this message as the people seek to live out these truths!

To have this happen once in my life is much more than I ever expected, but it has happened again. A second word from God that is just as powerful and will be just as life changing as the first one. I don't comprehend why God has chosen me to be the vessel by which this word has come. I only respond in obedience, saying, "Yes, Lord," I will be faithful and obedient to share this word all over the world, regardless of the cost!

This occurred in 2020, during the season of Covid-19 when lock downs and prohibitions of public meetings were in place. Rather than going to church on Sunday mornings, my wife and me, along with our children, participated in church services by live streaming as many other people were doing each week. There was one church and pastor we were drawn to who was quite powerful and successful. He pastored a large church, and the sermons were wonderful. We enjoyed the messages and often felt challenged in our Christian life and we were growing in our walk with the Lord Jesus Christ… then the worst happened.

The pastor was exposed in having an adulterous affair for the second time. What a tragedy for all connected to this ministry, however, that was not the worst of it. Two Sundays after the exposure, the plan was for him to address the church and all who watched remotely. He did address it very briefly, taking no responsibility for his actions, shifting blame on the other party, and presenting himself as just a victim resulting from past childhood issues and current pressures and that he just needed forgiveness. He then simply moved on and started preaching as normal. At the time of this writing, he is still preaching at a large church as if nothing occurred at all.

Having had issues in my past which I took full responsibility for and faced the consequences which I still walk out, I was in shock! My wife was considerably disturbed also and spoke out a brief word of prophecy which became a revelation to both of us...ultimately it became this once in a lifetime word from God that would be for all in this age!

My wife Mandy said, "this man has no fear of God!" The moment she stopped speaking it was like a bright light came on in my mind. It was like an explosion in my spirit and a revelation from God appeared in my heart as He said to me, "This has been your problem and is one of the greatest problems in the church today. There is little or no fear of Me in this world! Go, teach, and tell the people who will listen that every single problem that believers have is directly related to little or no fear of God in their lives!" I still shake in my soul to this day of the power in this word from God to me!

What you are about to read is the conclusion of three years of devoted study and teaching and a full and comprehensive search through the entire Bible to know everything we need to understand about the fear of God. As the subtitle of this book reads, "Are you afraid yet? You should be!" is the beginning of discovering and embracing a life where the fear of God is up front and central to our Christian lives! May the Lord help us to no longer live without the fear of God!

Here are three verses from the Bible to begin considering just from this introduction:

> **1. Ecclesiastes 12:13-14** *"Let us hear the conclusion of the whole matter: Fear God and keep His commandments, for this is man's all. For God will bring every work into judgment, including every secret thing, whether good or evil."*

> **2. Philippians 2:12-13** *"Therefore my beloved, as you have always obeyed, not as in my presence only, but now much more in my absence, work out your own salvation with fear and trembling; for it is God who works in you both to will and to do for His good pleasure."*

> **3. Matthew 10:28** *"And do not fear those who kill the body but cannot kill the soul. But rather fear Him who is able to destroy both soul and body in hell."*

An Important Note

IT IS SO AMAZING to me how a specific teaching like the fear of God just continues to expand as you grow in Christ. On any given day in my quiet times, God can reveal another insight related to the fear of God. The Word of God is so rich. Reading and studying it on a daily basis provides the Holy Spirit the opportunity to illuminate deeper truth regarding any topic and this is what He does for me constantly.

The important note that I want to speak to before you read any further is from a verse, I came across recently. It jumped off the page into my heart and after some thought and meditation, I realized it had great significance and could deepen your understanding as you read this book. Let's look at the verse found in Isaiah 29:13:

> *13 Therefore the Lord said: "Inasmuch as these people draw near with their mouths And honor Me with their lips, But have removed their hearts far from Me, And their fear toward Me is taught by the commandment of men,"*

I was struck by this verse when I read it. It is obviously focused on the fear of God. It reveals the important truth that unless the heart of a person is committed and close with God, all the "religious" verbiage coming out of the mouth is worthless. What spoke to me the most was the end of the verse, "and their fear toward Me is taught by the commandment of men."

The fear of the Lord that will be genuine and life-transforming is not simply what you'll read in this book. The information, inspiration, and guidance found in this book will have little value and produce little change in your life unless you embrace these truths with all your heart and soul, along with a drawing closer to God through genuine surrender on a daily basis.

It is not the information supplied by men coupled with a challenge and commandment by them to daily walk and live in the fear of God, it will be your heart that you freely surrender to the Holy Spirit to have a burning desire to live in the fear of God!

The important note here is that as you read this book, hopefully you will experience through surrender to God, a work of the Holy Spirit in your life. In other words, rather than just reading the text, you will experience a wonderful move of God in your heart. I hope you will join me in speaking from the depth of your soul, "I desire to draw nearer to God in my heart and allow the Holy Spirit to assist in teaching me the fear of God.!" ... Let us begin...

CHAPTER ONE:

The Comprehensive Definition of the Fear of God

AS WE DIVE into this awesomely important chapter, we need to consider what I call the **Four dangerous positions for a believer to be in during these present days of evil:**

- **Ignorance** – *You just don't know about something important.*

- **Distracted** – *You might know about something important but other things are more of a priority to you.*

- **Rebellion** – *You may know or not know about something important, but you just don't care or want anything to do with it.*

- **Deceived** – *You just know the wrong or partial information about something important.*

Each one of these can be a dangerous position. The fourth one is a place that so many Christian leaders and teachers are in. After so many years as a leader myself, travelling around the world in ministry, I see the reality of this everywhere. Please beware and seriously consider, lest you get stuck in one of these!

So, how would you define the fear of God? I have asked this question to numerous pastors, elders, Christian leaders, and Christians in general and normally the response has to do with a reverence for God. Many leaders actually say that it does not have anything to do with being afraid of God in any way. God is a God of love and forgiveness and through the death and resurrection of Jesus Christ there is no longer any need to be afraid of God. Often, I hear that we are living in the New Testament and no longer do Old Testament concepts of God apply to our lives.

At first thought, these arguments sound good but unfortunately several of the New Testament writers and even Jesus Himself totally disagrees with them. A serious examination of the writings in the New Testament upholds the same concept and theology found in the Old Testament related to who God is. In fact, we are told in Psalm 33:11 and in Hebrews 13:8, that God is the same yesterday, today, and forever and He never changes!

I believe that one of the main reasons there are so many failures morally, financially, emotionally, and spiritually in the Church and individual Christian's lives today is a lack of understanding and willingness to live daily in the fear of God. It does appear that as the world is becoming more ungodly, believers are following not far behind, and even entire denominations are struggling and dividing over clear scriptural teachings of what sin is and isn't… No fear of God! We just want to make up our own rules regardless of what the Bible teaches. We really could discuss for a long time how easy it is to drift away from God and His Word when the fear of God is misunderstood or just simply neglected altogether, but we won't at this time.

This of course begs the obvious question…What then is the fear of God? I can say it is much more in depth than you could realize. In a close examination of the entire Bible, we discover 180 verses that directly speak to the fear of God. There are so many others that indirectly refer to the fear of God, but we will only concentrate on what we can derive from the 180 direct verses. Chapter six provides a complete list of these verses so you can have them available in one place.

I believe we are ready to answer the question above, in a comprehensive fashion. There are seven features to the fear of God. Important to keep in mind is that although each feature is full in itself, each one is directly connected to the others to make a whole. In other words, you cannot separate one from the other without causing a faulty view or misunderstanding of the fear of God. We must carefully examine each feature individually and then understand the fear of God as a whole with seven parts. Much like a precious gem that might have seven sides. You can look at each side individually, but the gem's beauty and value are derived by the entirety of the gem. In addition, as you look at each feature, you can evaluate how much of this particular feature is active in your daily life. This now becomes the focus of how much work and attention you should be involved with in building up the features you find lacking in your daily life. Chapter seven provides a simple assessment tool to help you with this! So, let us get started:

The first feature of the fear of God is what I will label, **Awareness**. A fuller expression of this is an awareness of God's awesome continual presence around us and in us. Here are several scriptures that point to this specific feature: *2 Chronicles 19:5-7; 20:29; Nehemiah 1:11; Psalm 25:14; 34:7; 139:7-10; Acts 2:43; 9:31; Romans 8:9; 1 Corinthians 3:16.*

It is amazing how many Christians fail to realize that God is all around them and inside of them. God is Omni-present and exists everywhere at the same time. In the scriptures we discover a continual admonition from the Biblical writers to "seek" God. Often there are "woes" pronounced on people who choose not to seek Him (Isaiah 31:1 is an example). We don't have to seek Him or call upon Him for God to come be present with us, He already is there. The idea of seeking or calling on God is all about becoming "aware" of His presence. All of these listed scriptures speak directly to this. It is only through the fear of God that we become and remain so aware of His presence, because we are continuously seeking and calling out for Him. This only deepens our sensitivity to God's presence all around. As we increase the level of the fear of God in our lives, this awareness grows deeper!

Even more wonderful to perceive is that God the Holy Spirit permanently lives inside of every born-again believer. The salvation experience is all about the Holy Spirit coming to indwell us, never to leave us! Please realize that He is not sleeping or unaware of what's happening and going on in our minds and hearts and lives. He is fully aware, at all times. The problem is that we are not fully aware at all times that He is there. The fear of God is being aware that He is there inside of us and all around us. There is no place you can hide or escape His presence! Whatever you are thinking or doing when you are all alone or whatever, He is there, with you. Even in the worst of times, He is still there at work for your benefit. I can only imagine how the awareness of God's presence at all times with us and in us, could lead us to different and better decisions and outcomes in life. This is the first feature of the fear of God!

The second feature of the fear of God is what I will label, **Awe.** A fuller expression of this is a deep sense of awe, wonder, and respect of who God is and what He does. Here are several scriptures that point to this specific feature: *Psalm 5:7; 19:1-14… through creation and His Word Psalm 31;19; 33:8; 40:3; 64:9; 103:11,17; 118:4; Isaiah 6:1-8… through difficulties Acts 5:5,11; Revelation 1:9-20; 15:4*

You can almost see the connection to the first feature. As our awareness of God's presence increases and we see, hear, and experience God's presence and His work in us and around us, the only response from our hearts is awe and wonder of Him! Our reverence and respect towards Him grows and our praise and thanksgiving increases along with our worship deepening to new and wonderful levels. This feature of the fear of God is the one most recognized and spoken of by leaders. It is true and powerful, but it is only one of the seven features. Again, at this point, I can foresee believers making such better choices in life along with living with so much more joy and peace knowing God is God and is doing so much to make us more like Jesus and glorifying Himself in and through our lives! When we are able to have these awesome moments whether it's through creation or specific interventions of the Lord in our lives or those around us, we are left with that sense of how great is our God!

The third feature of the fear of God is what I label **Submission**. A fuller expression of this is a genuine connection and submission to Jesus as Lord as well as Savior of our life. Here are several scriptures that point to this specific feature: *Exodus 20:20; Deuteronomy 10:20; 13:4; 14:23; 17:19; Psalm 2:11; 85:9; Proverbs 8:13; John 15:1-11; 2 Corinthians 7:1,15; Colossians 2:6; Hebrews 11:7; 12:28; James 4:7*

The fear of the Lord brings us to a place that demands a decision. To be aware of Him and to be in awe and wonder of Him brings us face-to-face with that choice to either bow down and surrender to Him or to reject Him and walk away. The fear of God demands a decision of submission to Him as Lord and Savior.

Please understand that Jesus cannot be Savior if He is not Lord too. I have seen much confusion regarding this matter through the years. The whole concept of salvation involves getting connected to Christ through genuine submission of our life to Him. Jesus said very clearly in Mark 8:34-35, *"When He called the people to Himself, with His disciples also, He said to them "Whoever desires to come after Me, let him deny himself, and take up his cross, and follow Me. For whoever desires to save his life will lose it, but whoever loses his life for My sake and the gospel's will save it."* The other verses listed provide an additional basis to this point.

There is no theological unclarity in any of these passages. Either you surrender fully to Christ as your Lord, or you are not saved. There is no receiving Jesus as Savior and then later in life receiving Him as your Lord. The fear of God recognizes this clearly and as you are aware of Him and in awe of Him, submission to Him as Lord and Savior is naturally the next step in understanding what this fear really is!

The fourth feature of the fear of God is what I label **Honor**. A fuller expression of this is a commitment to honor, respect, glorify, and magnify Jesus in all that we do and think Here are several scriptures that point to this specific feature: *Deuteronomy 10:12; 1 Samuel 12:14,24; 2 Chronicles 19:9; Psalm 22:23; 135:20; Luke 5:26; 7:16; Acts 19:17; 1 Corinthians 10:31; Colossians 3:17*

Fearing God is directly related to honoring Him in all things. The verses given speak so powerfully to this issue. Please understand that I am writing believing that you have taken the time to read these verses of scripture, so you see the biblical foundation for each of these features. It is amazing to me how little heartfelt honor is given to Jesus in daily life. Just think about it, He is the Lord of creation, the God of the universe, the Alpha and Omega, the Bright and Morning Star, and so much more! As our God and Creator, how could we ever live without daily magnifying Him and honoring Him in all our thoughts and deeds? But when there is little or no fear of God, glorifying Him and honoring Him is the furthest thing from our mind and heart! Oh, my goodness, when I think of who He is to me and what He does constantly in me and around me… how I desire to honor, magnify, and glorify Him at all times… The fear of God operating in my life!

The distractions so prevalent in America and western cultures around the world, along with the demands from our cultures to gain more stuff, maintain our stuff, and just get ahead easily, keep our attention off of the Lord. I believe many Christians find it quite difficult to spend much time seriously considering who God is and how much He is at work in their lives. Thought processes of this nature are drowned out by the world, the flesh, and the devil. It is by living daily in the fear of God that we realize how important honoring, magnifying, and glorifying God is and actually practicing doing these specific actions as we are worshipping Him through the day! If we are too busy to honor God every day, we have little or no fear of God which will lead down dangerous paths.

The fifth feature of the fear of God is what I label **Accountability.** A fuller expression of this is an understanding and living out a lifestyle of our personal accountability to Him of our thoughts, motives, actions, and words. Here are several scriptures that point to this specific feature: *Genesis 3:10; Leviticus 19:14; 25:17,36,43; Deuteronomy 28:58; Nehemiah 5:9,15; Psalm 55:19; 115:13; Ecclesiastes 8:12; 12:13; Matthew 10:28; 1 Corinthians 3:11-15; 1 Timothy 5:20; 1 Peter 1:17; Revelation 20: 11-15*

This feature is the clearest one of the seven but is the most overlooked or rejected one of all. I find this incredibly sad in my heart and I am sure this is the reason for such failures, mistakes, and sins among Christian leaders and believers in general. It is time for a serious awakening among us all in understanding this feature and sincerely making application of it in our lives, not just periodically, but every single day! Walking and living daily in the fear of God!

This is so obvious in the above verses in both the Old Testament and the New Testament. In fact, the verses in the New Testament are even clearer and more enlightening. We must spend some time with this feature because of it's neglect and misunderstanding among so many leaders.

In discussing this, we must consider the balance of two truths. One truth is the finished work of Jesus on the cross for us. The second truth is the ongoing work of the Holy

Spirit living in us, helping us to deal with the current power of sin trying to lead us into bondage and overcoming us.

In the first truth of Jesus' finished work, He took our place and died as a sacrifice for all our sins. As we are drawn to Him by the conviction of the Holy Spirit and of our own free will we choose to surrender our lives to Christ as our Lord and Savior; we enter into His wonderful grace and forgiveness and we are born-again or as some refer to it, we are saved. This is a solid truth. But we must understand that this "salvation" we have entered has three phases. One is justification (the past) where the penalty of sin and the destiny of eternal death in Hell is removed. Second, is sanctification (the present) where the power of sin is currently being removed by the ongoing work of the Holy Spirit living in us. Third, is glorification (the future) where the presence of sin will be completely removed in the future when Jesus returns, and we receive our new resurrected bodies.

In understanding these three phases of salvation, we are able to grasp the second truth. The ongoing work of the Holy Spirit in our lives, helping us to deal with sin and its power to overcome us and bring us nothing but broken and sin-filled lives. "But I thought Jesus died for all our sins and now we never have to worry or be bothered by sin ever again," some might say.

It is a horrible mistruth to think that you never have to worry about sin again. It is unbiblical and seriously not supported by scripture at all. What we are forgiven of is the penalty of sin. We are justified by the death and resurrection of Christ, this is true, not that sin no longer is something to be bothered about. Just a casual reading through the New Testament provides evidence page after page of commands, admonitions, exhortations, pleadings, by every writer in the New Testament to deal with your sins, abstain from sins, be diligent to keep yourself from sins, confess your sins, and on and on. In other words, as a Christian, you must face the truth that sin problems are real and there is a constant battle with them. Thanks be to God for the Holy Spirit who is providing the power and guidance to be victorious over the power of sin in our lives, but don't be fooled for a moment that there is no struggle, the struggle is real!

So, we have clearly established the fact that sin for the Christian is a real problem. Christians can really sin today and without a continuous yielding surrender to the Holy Spirit, we will have major difficulties in this life and the next! It is the fear of God that brings us to the understanding that we will all be held to accountability for the way we live our lives, thoughts, words, and deeds. Living daily in the fear of God can make all the difference in the world.

To be sure we are on the same page of understanding, consider the following: Jesus Himself taught accountability through the parables of the talents. In the Book of Revelation 20:11-15, we find that with the Lamb's Book of Life, there are other "books." It is out of these "books" that all people will be judged. If you think this is only unbelievers, consider what Paul writes in 2 Corinthians 5:10 where he tells us that all believers will stand before the "Judgment

Seat of Christ" to give an account of their lives. In 1 Corinthians 3:11-15, we find Paul's clearest teaching concerning our accountability. In this passage, Paul is speaking to believers. He tells us there is only one foundation that can be in our lives and that foundation is Jesus Christ, our salvation. But we must be aware that we can build on that foundation with gold, silver, and precious stones or we can build with hay, wood, and stubble. Paul tells us that the Day of Judgment will be like fire to test our works, and we know what fire will do to hay, wood, and stubble. Paul makes a remarkable statement in verse 15, *"If anyone's work is burned, he will suffer loss; but he himself will be saved, yet so as through fire."* Paul indicates clearly that Christians will "suffer loss" in this judgment! Unfortunately, as Christians, our thoughts, deeds, and even our motives for doing what we do will be put to the test of fire some day!

The fear of God includes knowing and understanding that we will be held accountable for all our stuff. That fact alone should make every believer stay closer to God and live a godly life! Without the fear of God, a person doesn't even consider what they will be held accountable for in the day of judgment yet to come. Yes, we better be serious in dealing with our sinfulness and yes, we better be afraid!... The fear of God in operation.

The sixth feature of the fear of God is what I label **Word-Filled.** A fuller expression of this is a serious commitment to be devoted to His word. Here are several scriptures that point to this specific feature: *Deuteronomy 4:10; 5:29; 6:2,*

24; 8:6; 13:11; 31:12,13; 2 Chronicles 17:9-10; Psalm 86:11; 112:1; 119:38; Acts 2:42-43; John 8:31

I was raised in a Roman Catholic home in the 1950's and 1960's. Reading the Bible much less studying the Bible was not encouraged at all. In addition, I was told by the church that attempting to interpret the Bible by myself was forbidden and only the priests of the church were allowed to do that. Needless to say, the Bible had little or no contact or influence on my life. To be honest, I had no desire or knowledge of the scriptures. I became a believer on May 11, 1975, and immediately became a part of a Baptist church that encouraged reading, studying, and memorizing the scriptures, quite a new experience. In my early days as a Christian, I had an older pastor who told me something I have never forgotten. He said, "a key to a Spirit-filled life is to have a Word-filled life." He was so true!

Considering what the fear of God truly means, I have discovered that one of the seven features of the fear of God is to be seriously devoted to the Word of God. I can join my older brother in the Lord in saying that a Word-filled life is also a key to walking and living in the fear of God!

All of the verses listed above strongly speak to this matter of being devoted to God's word. It is amazing to me how clear this is. Not knowing what God's word has to say presents a problem in knowing who God is and what He desires for us and what He expects of us. After being a Christian and preaching and teaching God's word for almost 50 years, I still feel as if I am just getting started. The word of God is alive and powerful. It is always speaking to my heart in many ways as the Holy Spirit brings fresh illumination from it. Just a causal relationship with God's word is not really exercising the fear of God, there needs to be intense devotion to it!

In Acts 2:42-43, we read how the new believers there gave themselves to the word of God being devoted to what they were being taught by the Apostles and the end result was growth in the fear of God. Jesus is very clear in John 8:31, that if anyone wanted to be a disciple, they must "continue in His words." Devotion to the word of God provides the foundation and basis for the fear of God to grow in our life. It saddens my heart to see so many people coming to church without a Bible in their hand, much less how very few believers actually spend time every day in the word. I have heard a million excuses of why people just don't have the time anymore. Oh, my goodness, little or no devotion to the word has resulted in little or no fear of God in Christian's lives, no wonder believers far and wide are in so much trouble and are simply lukewarm in their Christian life.

Let me just state it loud and clear… "The fear of God is having a serious devotion to God's word, every day!"

The seventh and final feature of the fear of God is what I label **Humility**. A fuller expression of this is a commitment to walk in humility and be constantly crucifying our pride. Here are several scriptures that point to this specific feature: *Genesis 42:18; Leviticus 19:32; Joshua 24:14; Psalm 111:10; Proverbs 1:7; 15:16,33; 22:4; Galatians 2:20; Philippians 2:3-8,12; 1 Peter 3:15*

It is interesting to note that Proverbs 22:4 and 1 Peter 3:15 both link together the fear of God and humility. Please understand that these are not two different concepts, they really are the same, just providing a greater understanding of how a part of the fear of God is about living a life of humility. It goes without question that living a life of humility requires seriously dealing with pride.

The passage in Philippians 2:5ff is one of those *high watermarks* in the Bible. The example of humility that Christ modeled for us is specifically detailed in this passage. The purpose for Paul writing this was to urge every believer to live in the same way, which goes without saying that humility is a feature of the fear of God.

Pride is the sin that caused the devil and many angels to lose their place in heaven and pride is a dangerous sin in all of our lives also. Pride has a way of covering itself up, so we are the last to discover its presence and hold over us. Some may never make that discovery. The point I'm making here is that seeking to cultivate a spirit of humility in our lives will protect us from this danger. The fear of God demands the development of humility which includes the constant crucifying of our pride. Understand this is not simply an easy task to undertake. This can be hard work and, like a farmer plows his field every year to begin the process of re-planting, we must be willing to "plow" our hearts on a regular basis to continue living in this spirit of humility and the crucifying of our pride.

This final feature of the fear of God as connected to the others broadens our view and understanding of this important fear we are to live daily with. The danger here is to pick one or two of these and fool yourself into thinking, "I'm not doing so bad. I am doing a couple of these quite well and compared to others, I'm not half bad." I must insist that unless you have all seven of these features in operation to some extent, you are doing terrible! Yes, this is the whole point of this book, to confront us with the full truth and to challenge us to make a significant difference in how we are living out our lives.

How easy it would be to perform an exegesis on every scripture listed with each feature above to further deepen each point and demonstrate how vital and necessary each of these are to our walking and living in the fear of God every single day. As I stated earlier, every problem that a Christian will face is directly connected to the lack of the fear of God in one or more of these features. In all that I have to say in this book, do not lose sight of the fact that we need to seriously concentrate on working on these features in our lives. They do not occur naturally, nor do they develop and grow by themselves; we must work diligently on them, practicing them day after day. The more these are true and operating in our lives, the more success and power we will walk in through our lives. These seven areas are the crux of the matter. They are the center focus of our lives to walk and live in the fear of God!

So, the challenge before us is to honestly evaluate our lives in relation to these seven features. The evaluation/assessment tool is found in chapter seven. It might be a good idea to do your assessment now before going further, but you must be brutally honest with yourself. Not being honest will accomplish nothing for you. Once you are finished with the assessment, you will know how to pray for yourself and what features you need to dig into for some deep study and challenging yourself for genuine change so you can walk and live in the fear of God more than most!

The following chapters are only to provide insight, information, and motivation for living in the fear of God. Further enlightenment about this fear hopefully will encourage us to visit this chapter over and over again to provide the direction for our efforts. I believe that living in the fear of God is one of the most important lifestyles for the Christian today and this book is a genuine prophetic call to every believer to have a spiritual awakening to realize that we must all live and walk in the fear of God every single day!

Here is the outline in a summary:

Definition of the Fear of God

1. **Awareness:** An awareness of God's awesome continual presence around us and in us. 2 Chronicles 19:5-7; 20:29; Nehemiah 1:11; Psalm 25:14; 34:7; *139:7-10*; Acts 2:43; 9:31; *Romans 8:9*; *1 Corinthians 3:16*

2. **Awe:** A deep sense of awe, wonder, and respect of who God is and what He does. Psalm 5:7; *19:1-14... through creation and His Word* Psalm 31;19; 33:8; 40:3; 64:9; 103:11,17; 118:4; *Isaiah 6:1-8... through difficulties* Acts 5:5,11; *Revelation 1:9-20*; 15:4

3. **Submission:** Genuine connection and submission to Jesus as Lord as well as Savior of our life Exodus 20:20; Deuteronomy 10:20; 13:4; 14:23; 17:19; Psalm 2:11; 85:9; Proverbs 8:13; *John 15:1-11*; 2 Corinthians 7:1,15; *Colossians 2:6*; Hebrews 11:7; 12:28; *James 4:7*

4. **Honor:** A commitment to honor, respect, glorify, and magnify Jesus in all that we do and think. Deuteronomy 10:12; 1 Samuel 12:14,24; 2 Chronicles 19:9; Psalm 22:23; 135:20; Luke 5:26; 7:16; Acts 19:17; *1 Corinthians 10:31; Colossians 3:17;*

5. **Accountability:** An understanding and living out a lifestyle of our personal accountability to Him of our thoughts, motives, actions, and words. Genesis 3:10; Leviticus 19:14; 25:17,36,43; Deuteronomy 28:58; Nehemiah 5:9,15; Psalm 55:19; 115:13; Ecclesiastes 8:12; 12:13; Matthew 10:28; *1 Corinthians 3:11-15*; 1 Timothy 5:20; 1 Peter 1:17; *Revelation 20: 11-15*

6. **Word-Filled:** A serious commitment to be devoted to His word. Deuteronomy 4:10; 5:29; 6:2, 24; 8:6; 13:11; 31:12,13; 2 Chronicles 17:9-10; Psalm 86:11; 119:38; Acts 2:42-43; *John 8:31*

7. **Humility:** A commitment to walk in humility and be constantly crucifying our pride. Genesis 42:18; Leviticus 19:32; Joshua 24:14; Psalm 111:10; Proverbs 1:7; 15:16,33; 22:4; *Galatians 2:20*; *Philippians 2:3-8,12*; 1 Peter 3:15

CHAPTER TWO:

The Levels of the Fear of God

PEOPLE CAN EASILY FALL into the pitfall of thinking that everything is either "white or black." Life can be simpler with this philosophy but there are two problematic issues with this mindset. One is the simple truth that for most matters in this world, "things" often have numerous shades of gray. Our own perceptions have been proven to be skewed and can present various facts in the wrong way. My point here is that "white and black" thinking may be simpler, but it may lead you into wrong areas of thought. The second issue with this philosophy is that it can lead to a spirit of judgment, which is a dangerous position for a Christian to be in.

The fear of God is not as "white and black" as you might like it to be. In other words, there are levels of the fear of God. It is not just as simple as you either have the fear of God or you don't. The scriptures provide interesting insights into this matter. We discover several distinct levels at which people can be. This may indicate also that the possibility exists that there can be movement back and forth between these named levels. One way to understand the fear of God is that you may be at one of these levels or be moving forward or backward within them.

This is helpful as we periodically evaluate ourselves (not other people… the judgment issue) to see where we are at and what work we need to be involved with for improving and increasing our own fear of God. The assessment tool mentioned in chapter one and located in chapter seven will provide a picture of where you are within these levels. The tool is simple yet very insightful for self-evaluation.
Let's briefly identify and discuss the four named levels of the fear of God stated in the scriptures:

The first one is described quite clearly in Romans 3:9-18. We will call this one: <u>No Fear of God</u>. We see this in the scripture:

> [9] What then? Are we better than they? Not at all. For we have previously charged both Jews and Greeks that they are all under sin. [10] As it is written: "There is none righteous, no, not one; [11] There is none who understands; There is none who seeks after God. [2] They have all turned aside; They have together become

> unprofitable; There is none who does good, no, not one." ¹³ "Their throat is an open [d]tomb; With their tongues they have practiced deceit"; "The poison of asps is under their lips"; ¹⁴ "Whose mouth is full of cursing and bitterness." ¹⁵ "Their feet are swift to shed blood; ¹⁶ Destruction and misery are in their ways; ¹⁷ And the way of peace they have not known." ¹⁸ "There is no fear of God before their eyes."

Verse 18 provides a summary of the description of people who are given to these lifestyles and behavior, "there is no fear of God before their eyes." Without any fear of God, all manner of sinful attitudes and practices are evident. All seven features of the fear of God are missing and evil and sinfulness fills the minds, hearts, and lives of these people with little or no conviction.

Remember that movement between the levels of the fear of God is a reality. What is frightening to consider is the possibility that Christians can slide into this level as they give little or no attention to the fear of God. The results often become public in some way and are unfortunately reported through the news media, social media, and other forms of communication between people. As the old saying goes, "Bad news travels fast!" This of course leaves a path of untold hurt and devastation.

It does disturb most of us regarding how many Christian leaders "fall" on a regular basis. It seems like the three most common "falls" have to do with pride, greed, or sex. The most shocking fact is that for everyone you do hear about, there are so many others you don't hear about, and there are even more that are "falling" secretly in their hearts and minds with little, or nothing being done to correct it. Living in the level of no fear of God, what a serious and dangerous place to be!

The second level is what we will call: <u>Little Fear of God</u>. This is found described in 2 Kings 17:28-41:

> *²⁸ Then one of the priests whom they had carried away from Samaria came and dwelt in Bethel, and taught them how they should fear the LORD. ²⁹ However every nation continued to make gods of its own, and put them in the shrines on the high places which the Samaritans had made, every nation in the cities where they dwelt. ³⁰ The men of Babylon made Succoth Benoth, the men of Cuth made Nergal, the men of Hamath made Ashima, ³¹ and the Avites made Nibhaz and Tartak; and the Sepharvites burned their children in fire to Adrammelech and Anammelech, the gods of Sepharvaim. ³² So they feared the LORD, and from every class they appointed for themselves priests of the [a]high places, who sacrificed for them in the shrines of the high places. ³³ They feared the LORD, yet served their own gods—according to the rituals of the nations from among whom they were carried away. ³⁴ To this day they continue practicing the former rituals; they do not fear the LORD, nor do they follow their statutes or their ordinances, or the law and commandment which the LORD had commanded the chil-*

*dren of Jacob, whom He named Israel, * *35 with whom the* LORD *had made a covenant and charged them, saying: "You shall not fear other gods, nor bow down to them nor serve them nor sacrifice to them; 36 but the* LORD, *who brought you up from the land of Egypt with great power and an outstretched arm, Him you shall fear, Him you shall worship, and to Him you shall offer sacrifice. 37 And the statutes, the ordinances, the law, and the commandment which He wrote for you, you shall be careful to observe forever; you shall not fear other gods. 38 And the covenant that I have made with you, you shall not forget, nor shall you fear other gods. 39 But the* LORD *your God you shall fear; and He will deliver you from the hand of all your enemies." 40 However they did not obey, but they followed their former rituals. 41 So these nations feared the* LORD, *yet served their carved images; also their children and their children's children have continued doing as their fathers did, even to this day.*

Verses 33 and 41 tell us that the people "feared the Lord" but continued to serve other gods. This may sound like they had no fear of God but please give them a little credit. It says they did fear the Lord too in both verses. Now obviously this is not acceptable, but it is amazing how many people who call themselves Christians have Jesus Christ in one hand and the world (other gods) in the other hand. In the New Testament we find several of the writers addressing believers who are struggling with following Christ and loving the world too. It didn't work in the Old Testament, and it doesn't work in the New Testament. Do not think for a moment that it works today either!

Having a Little Fear of God is like being "lukewarm," as found in the Book of Revelation 3:14-16. It makes God sick to His stomach and causes God to vomit you out of His mouth! This is a serious matter to consider and for any genuine follower of Christ, it should be considerable motivation to work diligently to move out of that level quickly! As with the level of no fear of God, lifestyles and attitudes are going to be corrupt and short-sighted and will result in lots of people being hurt and big messes to clean up. When I consider all of this, it sheds some light on what is happening to so many leaders in the Christian world today. After all, when someone "falls" in leadership we normally ask the question, "What happened?" Considering this discussion of a Little Fear of God is providing some strong clues to the answer.

The third level of the fear of God is what we will call: <u>The Normal Ongoing Fear of God</u>. This is the level that we find in the scriptures in which we are called, commanded, and admonished to walk in daily. This is a level to achieve and maintain to the best of our ability. This involves all seven features being, to some extent active and growing in a Christian's life. Attention is being given to all seven of the features and honest and sincere work is being accomplished in developing, maintaining, and growing these areas. The blessings and results of living in this fear of God is addressed in detail in the following chapters.

It is amazing to see how believer's lives begin to change for the better once they understand and diligently walk in this wonderful fear of God. Perspectives, attitudes, lifestyles, and the total outlook on life is much healthier and more positive. The need for the Ongoing Fear of God in every believer's life is crucial and absolutely necessary, especially in this day and age. Just consider this one verse in Psalm 128:1:

"Blessed is everyone who fears the LORD, Who walks in His ways."

The fourth and final level of the fear of God as stated in the scripture is: <u>More Fear than Most.</u> We find this stated in Nehemiah 7:1-2:

"1 Then it was, when the wall was built and I had hung the doors, when the gatekeepers, the singers, and the Levites had been appointed, 2that I gave the charge of Jerusalem to my brother Hanani, and Hananiah the leader of the citadel, for he was a faithful man and feared God more than many."

It is exciting to know that you can excel in your personal fear of the Lord, reaching a level where you can achieve More Fear than Most. This is not an easy level to reach but it is possible. As you would consider this, be assured that the rewards and blessings are increased too. Please understand that to have this level of the fear of God does not eliminate persecution, trials, and difficulties. I can say with confidence that the troubles and difficulties actually work towards the development of such a strong level of the fear of God. In our post-modern age of Christianity there is way too much emphasis and teaching on a "prosperity" for the faithful which seems to eliminate any real trouble in life. Honestly, examining the scriptures reveals that the opposite is true, and a strong clear theology of troubles and suffering is essential for true spiritual growth, if our response is to be godly!

Summarizing this chapter, there are a few matters to emphasize. First of all, there are four distinct levels identified in the scriptures of the fear of God:

1. No Fear of God
2. Little Fear of God
3. Normal Ongoing Fear of God
4. More Fear than Most

Second, the level of the fear of God a person has can be built up or it can be slowly drained away. There is not an "on and off" switch so that it can occur quickly. It is more of a process that can be quite slow at times. This presents a danger because one might not be aware that the fear of God is slowly draining out of their life by their distracted focus or other issues demanding attention in their life.

Finally, building up and maintaining a higher level of the fear of God will require sincere attention, commitment, and hard work on our part.

With these matters in mind, we can say that the fear of God is a constant state of being, a prevailing attitude of the heart, and a continuous experience of life that we work diligently at developing and maintaining the highest level we can!

CHAPTER THREE:

The Characteristics of Those Who Fear God

AS WE BEGIN THIS CHAPTER, there are a couple of things to understand and consider. First of all, and most importantly, we must not view these characteristics as goals to work toward. These characteristics are the natural overflow in a person's life who is fearing God. We should focus all our attention on the seven features of the fear of God, to spend our time and effort improving. These characteristics only provide us a reflection of the level of fear operating in our lives. If it's hard to see any of these or the opposite characteristics are manifesting in our life, then it reveals a problem, and we should place effort on the seven features to seek to correct it.

In the second place as mentioned above, we will examine the characteristics closely but also realize that with little or no fear of God in our life, the opposites will be true. If we were to examine the fruit from an orange tree, we would expect to find certain things. If we didn't find those expected characteristics that make up a healthy orange, we would determine it is either not an orange or an unhealthy orange at best.

A third consideration is that the list provided here is not completely exhaustive. We will examine twelve specific characteristics in this chapter as well as considering some thoughts of their opposites. There very well may be other characteristics that you might find in the scriptures other than these twelve. This chapter is an attempt to provide enough characteristics for all of us to get a full picture of what a life looks like that fears God well. Finding others through your own personal study just reveals that you are exercising the sixth feature of fearing God by being devoted to the Word of God! With these three matters in mind, let's jump in!

The First Characteristic

<u>Those who fear God ongoing will experience and have regular intimacy with the Lord.</u>

Consider Psalm 25:14, "*The secret of the LORD is with them that fear him; and he will show them his covenant.*"

The Hebrew word we find here for "secret" has to do with personal and intimate conversations that very close friends may have. The emphasis is not on some secret information that no one else knows, but on the intimate and closeness one can have with the Lord. It is sad that so many believers do not have a real intimate relationship with the Lord involving such close communication with Him. The result of fearing God provides this wonderful closeness, and the Lord is able to reveal such marvelous truth to a person.

Not having much fear of God, a person only experiences a casual or superficial relationship and communication with God. In addition, God may feel like a million miles away, especially in troubled times. The scripture could be reworded to reflect the opposite, "*The secret of the Lord is nowhere to be found with those who have little, or no fear of God and He will not show them His covenant.*"

Those who fear God well experience and have regular intimacy with the Lord.

The Second Characteristic

Evil is not an option or a consideration in the life of one who fears God well.

Consider Job 1:1, *"There was a man in the land of Uz, whose name was Job; and that man was blameless and upright, and one who feared God and shunned evil."*

The verse doesn't say that Job was perfect. We discover that truth later in the book. It does say that he was "blameless and upright" and that because of his fear of God he "shunned evil." The Hebrew word here for "shunned" means to turn aside or to turn away from following a particular course leading to danger. It can also mean to turn into a place of shelter or refuge. The idea coming out of this word is that evil and the evil way is not an option to consider for the person who is fearing God. The fear of God results in turning away from potential evil and finding safe refuge. We can understand that the shelter we desire is both the Lord Jesus Christ and the power of the Holy Spirit to help us.

With little or no fear of God, the opposite is true. Evil is not only an option, but too often the real desire of someone's heart. Faced with temptation, consideration gives the temptation room to take root in our hearts. The love for gossip or lustful thoughts related to sex, money, and possessions, along with bad thoughts towards others, prevails more in our hearts and minds then we would like to admit. The question that quickly arises is what do we desire, sin and satisfaction of our flesh or do we desire the safe refuge and shelter of Christ to turn into when temptation comes?

Evil is not an option or a consideration in the life of one who fears God.

The Third Characteristic

<u>The person who fears God well, takes responsibility for his life and the mistakes he makes and doesn't blame God or others.</u>

Consider Job 1:22, *"In all this Job did not sin nor charge God with wrong."*

The Hebrew word "charge" here simply means to lay the blame at the feet of another. There is so much wrong with our world. There are so many difficulties that can come to our lives. Some of these problems are of our own making and some are the results of what others do to us. In addition, we seem to live in a culture where everyone wants to blame someone else for what's wrong or what goes wrong in their life. But the person who walks and lives in the fear of God is ready to take responsibility for their sins and mistakes, no matter how painful it may be, and they never desire to blame God for the problems of their life.

The person with little or no fear of God in their life will always find someone to blame for their problems. God is an easy target to lay blame on too. I have actually known a few people, who claimed to be Christians, who seemed to be experts at blaming and shaming others; holding anyone else responsible for their sins, mistakes, and troubled times they experience in life, rather than taking any responsibility for themselves.

The person who fears God takes responsibility for his life and the mistakes he makes, not blaming God or others. The level of fearing God in one's life will determine the extent of his or her taking this responsibility seriously.

The Fourth Characteristic

<u>Those who fear God well set their mind and heart on God seeking to live a holy life.</u>

Consider Isaiah 26:3, *"You will keep him in perfect peace, Whose mind is stayed on You, Because he trusts in You."* Also consider Colossians 3:1, *"If then you were raised with Christ, seek those things which are above, where Christ is, sitting at the right hand of God."*

It is always amazing to me to discover how few believers seriously are seeking God to live a holy life. Obviously, we understand from scripture that God is our source of a holy life; this is not something we can produce within ourselves. The Bible says that "there is no good thing in our flesh." Our old self is bound and determined to live selfishly regardless of what sins are required to obtain fulfillment, which never actually comes.

Fearing God leads us to look to Him as our basis, our foundation, our source, and our example of a holy lifestyle. Those who fear God "set" their mind and heart on God.

"Setting" our mind and heart on God is about making Him a priority as we are submitted to Him as our Lord and Master (these are elements of the definition of fearing God). This is not just an occasional occurrence, it's a characteristic of a daily lifestyle. It is as noticeable as a beautiful sunrise or sunset that happens every day!

Little or no fear of God demonstrates itself in the absence of this pursuit of God. There is little or no desire to walk down this avenue. There may be an occasion when some conviction might arise from exposure of mistakes or just going to church where a piercing sermon may prod one to seek God or live a holy life, but without the genuine and ongoing fear of God, this is just a passing desire soon to be forgotten or put behind you as the world and evil lures you on into self-interests and deception. Of course, the Word of God has little or no place in your life to be an encouragement or correction of lifestyle.

The Fifth Characteristic

<u>Those who fear God well honor and delight in the Word of God.</u>

Consider Psalm 112:1, *"Praise the Lord! Blessed is the man who fears the Lord, Who delights greatly in His commandments."*

There could be quite a large number of verses to share with this point, but we will consider just this one. The verse indicates that the result or the characteristic of one who fears the Lord "delights greatly" in the Word of God. It is interesting that it says "greatly" not just simply "delights." "Greatly" here shows how deep and far reaching this desire is. In other words, the one who fears God well is in love with the Word of God. It is vitally important to them and is a huge priority in their life. No one has to encourage them or constantly direct them to be in the Word. It's like air to breathe and food to eat. Every day there is the hunger and thirst for the Word of God.

When there is little or no fear of God in someone's life, the Word of God is more of a burden than a blessing. Reading or studying the Word is often a chore to perform and is boring at best. Little or no fresh illumination from the Holy Spirit ever flows out of the Word to them. For the most part, the Word is either misunderstood or not even understood at all. It is definitely not on the daily list of things to do, much less desperately needed to even face the day.

I really need to ask some questions at this point in your reading: Is the Bible, God's Word to you? Is it a decoration around the house, a symbol of your religious piety when you go to church? Or is it your lifeblood and the most important possession you have which you "greatly desire" at all times?... I think you know what I'm getting at!

The Sixth Characteristic

<u>Those who fear God well have no problem being submitted to others and Obeying God.</u>

Consider these three verses:

Genesis 22:12, "And He said, "Do not lay your hand on the lad, or do anything to him; for now I know that you fear God, since you have not withheld your son, your only son, from Me."

Colossians 3:22-25, <u>22</u> Bondservants, obey in all things your masters according to the flesh, not with eyeservice, as men-pleasers, but in sincerity of heart, fearing God. <u>23</u> And whatever you do, do it heartily, as to the Lord and not to men, <u>24</u> knowing that from the Lord you will receive the reward of the inheritance; for you serve the Lord Christ. <u>25</u> But he who does wrong will be repaid for what he has done, and there is no partiality.

Hebrews 12:28, "Therefore, since we are receiving a kingdom which cannot be shaken, let us have grace, by which we may serve God acceptably with reverence and godly fear."

Here is another characteristic that is so forth telling of how little or no fear of God is among believers and the church today. After almost 50 years in the ministry, I have seen one of the worst problems in Christian's lives is the lack of submission and the desire for selfish control over others; seeking either recognition and/or power. It has caused untold church splits, wounded hearts, and seemingly irreparable damage to the cause of Christ! What is so tragic is that this is simply the lack of the fear of God in Christian's hearts. This tragedy could begin reversal immediately if the fear of God was infused into believer's lives today! And this also has to do with obeying God, not for selfish reasons or when only it's convenient but just genuinely from the heart obeying God because He is God!

The Seventh Characteristic

Those who fear God are surrendered to, committed to, and faithful to God with genuine humility.

Consider these three scriptures:

Jeremiah 44:10, "They have not been humbled, to this day, nor have they feared; they have not walked in My law or in My statutes that I set before you and your fathers."

Nehemiah 7:2, "that I gave the charge of Jerusalem to my brother Hanani, and Hananiah the leader of the citadel, for he was a faithful man and feared God more than many."

Philippians 2:12, "Therefore, my beloved, as you have always obeyed, not as in my presence only, but now much more in my absence, work out your own salvation with fear and trembling."

In these verses the message is loud and clear. Believers who fear God are characterized by their surrender, commitment, and faithfulness to God with genuine humility in their lives. Jeremiah indicates that their level of fear toward God is directly connected to their humility. In Nehemiah the same thing is true as related to faithfulness. In fact, this man named here in the passage feared God more than many did and that was resulting from his faithfulness to God. Paul speaks of "working out our salvation" in godly fear. This is clearly related to the whole matter of surrender, commitment, and faithfulness. These matters are what describe our salvation being "worked" out.

It is easy to see how this particular characteristic speaks loudly of the level of fear towards God one might have. We do live in an age where these three matters are greatly lacking in Christian's lives. The selfishness of Christians demonstrates just how lacking we are of the fear of God. It is a shame, but this provides a window into our own souls of the emptiness and absence of a genuine and honest fear of God.

I have myself as a pastor, and I have heard so many other Christian leaders preach on, teach about, or share how frustrated they are that their people have such little surrender, commitment, and faithfulness. This has resulted in untold amounts of messages and designed programs to raise people's commitment and faithfulness. We as leaders, need to see that the lack of these three matters is a result of little or no fear of God in their hearts. When believers begin to fear God and grow in their fear of God, the direct result will be a heightened level of surrender, commitment, and faithfulness to Jesus!

I can only say to every leader reading this: teach and lead your people to fear God, make fearing God a priority and you will see the miraculous change in your people as they are being surrendered to Jesus, being committed to Jesus, and being faithful to Jesus! Fearing God is the center of attention for change.

The Eighth Characteristic

Those who fear God find awe and wonder on a regular basis in who God is and His handiwork all around them.
Consider Psalm 19:1-6:

"1 To the Chief Musician. A Psalm of David. The heavens declare the glory of God; And the firmament shows His handiwork. 2 Day unto day utters speech, And night unto night reveals knowledge. 3 There is no speech nor language Where their voice is not heard. 4 Their line has gone out through all the earth, And their words to the end of the world. In them He has

set a tabernacle for the sun 5 Which is like a bridegroom coming out of his chamber, And rejoices like a strong man to run its race. 6 Its rising is from one end of heaven, And its circuit to the other end; And there is nothing hidden from its heat."

We could literally quote dozens of scriptures to prove this point, but just this one will do. Whether we are gazing at the stars at night or examining the intricacies of the human cell through a microscope, we see the handiwork of God and we are full of awe and wonder. Considering the make-up of the human body or any other organic or even inorganic thing, we are awestruck with God's glory! The images of stars and galaxies sent back by space-borne telescopes can take our breath away because we are seeing the majesty of our great God, the creator of all things!

Without the fear of God, there is no awe of God and His handiwork; there is no wonder at all. Men without the fear of God have made up and continue to make up all manner of explanations of these things and theorize how they came to be, giving little or no thought to God Almighty and Jesus Christ who made everything in the universe!

The fear of God doesn't take away the scientific study and research of these things, it only enhances the awe and wonder of God Himself in how He has made these things and caused them to be in perfect order and union with the entire universe. Behind every new discovery and image, the glory of God is magnified and for those who fear Him, we are left breathless!

The Ninth Characteristic

<u>Those who fear God live a blessed and contented life.</u>
Consider Psalm 128:1-4:

> "*1 A Song of Ascents. Blessed is everyone who fears the Lord, Who walks in His ways. 2 When you eat the labor of your hands, You shall be happy, and it shall be well with you. 3 Your wife shall be like a fruitful vine In the very heart of your house, Your children like olive plants All around your table. 4 Behold, thus shall the man be blessed Who fears the Lord.*"

As with each of these characteristics, there are many scriptures both in the Old and New Testament that can be quoted, but this one incorporates the complete idea. When a person is striving to fear God with as much depth as possible and is continually growing in his fear, his life will be seen as a blessed life. For sure he will have a measure of contentment that cannot be found in others who do not fear God or who fear God very little.

It is important to see that this passage indicates that even this man's family are recipients of the blessings and contentment. Obviously, this doesn't take away the family's responsibility to follow the Lord too. It is understood that as the father's heart is so set on fearing God, he would do all he can to lead his family in the same way. Common sense along with other scriptural teachings bears this out. The idea this passage demonstrates is just how much blessing and contentment will be experienced when people are fearing God in a meaningful way.

Again, it's important to point out that this is a *natural result* of the hard work of fearing God taken from the seven-fold definition of fearing God, not that we try to work on the characteristic.

When I see so many Christians, clergy and lay people expressing such discontent and always in desperate need of blessing, I can't help but wonder where the fear of God is in their lives. The truth of this characteristic is clear and unfortunately the normal experience of the life of one who doesn't fear God has little or no blessing or contentment in life. Hopefully by now, each of us reading this book is sensing some serious conviction from the Holy Spirit and there is becoming an ever-increasing urgency to start building our fear of God!

The Tenth Characteristic

<u>Those who fear God demonstrate through their lifestyles that they walk in the Fear of the Lord.</u>
Consider Psalm 60:4:

*"You have given a banner to those who fear You,
That it may be displayed because of the truth."*

This characteristic is natural. If someone fears God, then their life will reflect that walk. But this characteristic can reveal whether it's just the right words being spoken or if it is genuine. I have to admit it is easy to learn the correct verbiage in Christian matters but not truly walk the talk. I think more of us are guilty of this than we might like to admit. This characteristic becomes a telltale sign of the truth of walking daily in the fear of God.

The verse indicates that there is a "banner" or a flag waving over those who fear God. It is an ensign that provides clarity of that which we have and walk. It is displayed, up and waving because of the truth of the matter. I enjoy watching college football because of the intensity of the game along with the intensity of the fans! They come with their costumes, flags, and other gear to clearly demonstrate who their team is, and they often wave their gear to prove the point. Those who daily walk in the fear of God also have their "banners" that demonstrate clearly the truth of their walk with God in fear.

Those who do not really fear God much in their lives, display other "banners." Their lifestyles show a different allegiance, one that doesn't include the fear of God. Their loyalty and interests are in other directions and their lives not only demonstrate that but also the number of problems and difficulties they are constantly struggling with show it too.

The Eleventh Characteristic

<u>Those who fear God help the local churches grow and multiply.</u>
Consider Acts 9:31:

> "Then the churches throughout all Judea, Galilee, and Samaria had peace and were edified. And walking in the fear of the Lord and in the comfort of the Holy Spirit, they were multiplied."

The local church is right in the heart of God. All through the New Testament we see and read over and over again how God loves His Church and desires for it to grow and multiply. Jesus in the Great Commission, commands us to share the gospel, baptize believers, and disciple believers all over the world. In one verse in Matthew, Jesus tells us that "the gates of hell will not prevail against the church." Jesus loves the church and gave His life for it.

When believers are walking in the fear of God, they carry the desire of the Lord in them to love the church and to help it to grow and multiply. Looking at the above verse in Acts, we see this very thing. The basis of the growth and multiplication was the fear of God. Please don't miss this.

Unfortunately, what I see today is the majority of believers are more interested in what the church can do for them rather than what they can do for the church! This is often the criteria by which a church is chosen to go to. The really sad thing is that the larger the church grows, the more this is true. And church leaders are always trying to figure out how to lead their people to be more committed to the church and take on more responsibilities. Some statisticians have authored reports that indicate that 20% of any congregation does 80% of the work and giving. So, leaders are always thinking and designing innovative programs and gimmicks to get more people involved in the work of the church.

Here is the truth of the matter. Here is the answer to how to accomplish this… lead people into fearing God!!! Not just a little but to learn how to fear God more than most! Those who fear God freely with sincerity are willing and volunteering to help in any way they can. There is no need to manipulate church members in any way, when they grow in their fear of God, they will hunger to serve the Lord in any way they can in the church!

All I can say at this point is "he who has ears to hear, let him hear what the Spirit is saying to the church" and to leadership!

The Twelfth Characteristic

Those who fear God discover that changing ungodly and sinful thoughts and behaviors is not a difficult or impossible matter.

Consider Psalm 55:19,

"God will hear, and afflict them, Even He who abides from of old. Selah Because they do not change, Therefore they do not fear God."

As with all the other characteristics, there could be dozens of scriptures provided to make the points, but I give you just one or two along the way. I am surprised by how many Christians have either stated or truly believe in their hearts that change for them is so difficult or even impossible. I have to admit, I have felt and thought this way about certain thoughts and behaviors in my own life. I do realize that I am not alone. In my counseling ministry, I have lost count of the people who have honestly confessed this very thing. I have wondered and pondered for many years if this might be true, but in discovering the truth about fearing God, I can now testify with a loud resounding voice that change is really possible!!!

In fact, having and walking in the fear of God makes it easier than you could ever think. This is true! Change is possible and it's not half as difficult as you might think. Look closely at the verse above. The reason for no change is because they have no fear of God. When you consider the elements of the fear of God and you are constantly making your focus and your work on maintaining and increasing the fear of God in your life, the truth of this characteristic will be a reality in your life!

Of course, the opposite is true. Little or no fear of God will prove to make change extremely difficult or even impossible. Again, look at the verse above.

As we conclude this chapter, I want you to consider the three points I discussed in the introduction. I don't want to belabor them again except just to mention them in closing. First of all, these characteristics are only a reflection of the level of the fear of God you have in your life. They should not be the focus of activity to improve, the focus should be on the seven-fold definition of the fear of God. Second, that the opposites of these are true in those who have little or no fear of God. Thirdly, these twelve characteristics are not exhaustive by any means. As you are devoted to the Word of God, you will find others to add to these.

I can only pray that as you read and consider these twelve, that it will be like a mirror for you, reflecting what is true in your heart and your walk if fearing God is a priority or not for you!

CHAPTER FOUR:

The Benefits and Consequences of Fearing or Not Fearing God

IN BEGINNING THIS CHAPTER, I believe it is important to once again consider the four dangerous positions in which believers can fall into in these days of evil:

- Ignorance – You just don't know about something important.
- Distracted – You might know about something important but other things are more of a priority to you.

- **Rebellion – You may know or not know about something important, but you just don't care or want anything to do with it.**
- **Deceived – You just know the wrong or partial information about something important.**

Each one of these is a dangerous position to be in. The fourth one is a place that too many Christian leaders and teachers are in. After so many years as a leader myself, travelling around the world in ministry, I see the reality of this everywhere. Please be aware and seriously consider, lest you get stuck in one of these positions!

We spend time, effort, and prayer in building the fear of the Lord in our lives through focusing on the seven features. It wouldn't hurt to rehearse them again over in our mind. As these features grow and are built up in our lives, we have naturally flowing out of our lives, the characteristics discussed in the last chapter. If these characteristics are weak or lacking in ourselves, we need to spend more time building these features rather than getting sidetracked by trying to work on improving the characteristics.

Now, once we have these seven features growing and stable in our lives, the results will be demonstrated through the benefits in the life of a person that fears the Lord more than most. Obviously, the opposite consequences will be reality for those who have little or no fear of God. We will focus our discussion on twelve clear benefits or consequences derived from fearing or not fearing God. You will possibly discover other ones in addition to these twelve as you continue to be devoted to the Word of God so, please don't think that this is an exhaustive list.

1. Fearing or not fearing God prolongs or shortens the time of a person's life.

Consider these scriptures:

> *Deuteronomy 5:33 "You shall walk in all the ways which the Lord your God has commanded you, that you may live and that it may be well with you, and that you may prolong your days in the land which you shall possess."*

> *Deuteronomy 6:2 "that you may fear the Lord your God, to keep all His statutes and His commandments which I command you, you and your son and your grandson, all the days of your life, and that your days may be prolonged."*

> *Psalm 34:11-12 "Come, you children, listen to me; I will teach you the fear of the Lord. Who is the man who desires life, And loves many days, that he may see good?"*

> *Proverbs 10:27 "The fear of the Lord prolongs days, But the years of the wicked will be shortened."*

> *Ecclesiastes 7:17-18 "Do not be overly wicked, Nor be foolish: Why should you die before your time? Is good that you grasp this, And also not remove your hand from the other; For he who fears God will escape them all".*
>
> *Ecclesiastes 8:12-13 "Though a sinner does evil a hundred times, and his days are prolonged, yet I surely know that it will be well with those who fear God, who fear before Him. But it will not be well with the wicked; nor will he prolong his days, which are as a shadow, because he does not fear before God."*
>
> *Hebrews 9:27 "And as it is appointed for men to die once, but after this the judgment,"*

For most of my life, I believed there was a designated time for each of us to die and there was nothing you could do to change that. I often used the above verse from Hebrews as my proof text. I was wrong! I was seriously wrong! Through this intensive study of the fear of God in the scriptures, I have come to a strong biblical conviction that the opposite is true. Yes, there is an appointed time, but you can either add to or you can take away from that appointed time.

This truth provides the basis for serious comfort for those who have lost loved ones who have feared God in their lives. Now I take the position that young children are in a state of innocence which I believe includes the fear of God being innate within them, or what is provided to them through their parents covering because of their fear of God. So, when someone dies regardless of the cause or reason of death, if there is the fear of God, then they have lived longer than their appointed time to die. This does not take away any of the sadness or grief, but it does provide some comfort that they were able to live longer than originally set. Thank you Lord for a few more days, weeks, months, or years! Unfortunately, the opposite is true also. Living without the fear of God will shorten the days of a person's life. Now that is sad! Consider with me the matter of abortion. I do realize how culturally controversial this matter is. But you cannot turn your mind and heart away from the fact that conception begins at birth and abortion is murder, a gross sin. The life of these children has ended long before their appointed time because the parents and/or others involved chose not to fear God and to do what they wanted, the sin of murder for convenience!

As we read and understand these listed scriptures, we see the truth very clearly. Each cries out to us to live a life of fearing God. I have done more funerals than I care to remember. In almost every one of them the expressed desire of those loved ones left is, "I wish there was more time."

The wonderful, good news to each of us is, "Fear God" and you will prolong your days. We can actually live longer! Praise the Lord! Fear Him!

The opposite is true also for those who do not fear the Lord. Their life will be shortened, by days, weeks, months, or even years. Living a life with no fear of God, where you abuse or misuse your body through alcohol, drugs, tobacco, poor nutrition, sex outside of marriage, and so many other things too numerous to mention will guarantee a shortened lifespan and that is what can cause great grief and sadness for those who are left! Again, fear God!

2. Fearing God produces a quality of life and experiencing God's love, favor, and mercy. Not fearing God lessens the quality of life and experiencing God's love, favor, and mercy.

Consider all these scriptures:

Proverbs 14:27: "The fear of the Lord is a fountain of life, To turn one away from the snares of death."

Proverbs 15:16: "Better is a little with the fear of the Lord, Than great treasure with trouble."

Proverbs 19:23: "The fear of the Lord leads to life, And he who has it will **abide** *in satisfaction; He will not be* **visited** *with evil."*

Proverbs 22:4: "By humility and the fear of the Lord Are riches and honor and life."

Psalms 31:19: "Oh, how great is Your goodness, Which You have laid up for those who fear You,

Which You have prepared for those who trust in You In the presence of the sons of men!"

Psalms 33:18-19: "Behold, the eye of the Lord is on those who fear Him, On those who hope in His mercy, To deliver their soul from death, And to keep them alive in famine."

Psalms 34:9: "Oh, fear the Lord, you His saints! There is no want to those who fear Him."

Psalms 103:11,13,17: " <u>11</u> For as the heavens are high above the earth, So great is His mercy toward those who fear Him; <u>13</u> As a father pities his children, So the Lord pities those who fear Him. <u>17</u> But the mercy of the Lord is from everlasting to everlasting On those who fear Him, And His righteousness to children's children,"

Psalms 115:13: "He will bless those who fear the Lord, Both small and great."

Psalms 145:19: "He will fulfill the desire of those who fear Him; He also will hear their cry and save them."

Isaiah 33:6: "Wisdom and knowledge will be the stability of your times, And the strength of salvation; The fear of the Lord is His treasure."

Malachi 4:2: "But to you who fear My name The Sun of Righteousness shall arise With healing in His wings; And you shall go out And grow fat like stall-fed calves."

Luke 1:50: "And His mercy is on those who fear Him From generation to generation."

There are so many scriptures that speak to this issue. I have printed them out here so you can read them carefully and spend some quality time meditating on them. It would be easy to preach a sermon on each one of these passages; they are so clear and speak so loudly. There is no doubt from these verses, Fearing God produces a quality of life along with experiencing God's love, favor, and mercy on a regular basis. Just printing them and reading them again creates a desire in my own heart to sincerely improve and increase my fear of the Lord.

Just a little exegesis on a couple of verbs found in Proverbs 19:23, which speak strongly to the continuous nature of this matter of fearing God. "**Abide**" is an imperfect verb (continuous action). "**Visited**" is an imperfect verb too and means "not to have rule over me or move me or have oversight over me!" So, this is not something we do periodically or when we receive some conviction from a message or what not, this is a pursuit of life… a lifestyle!

On the other hand, not regularly fearing God lessens the quality of life and the possibility of experiencing God's love, favor, and mercy on any qualitative basis. A clear understanding of this provides incredible insight into why so many people, including believers, are having such difficulties on a regular basis in their lives actually doubting if God loves them, has any favor, or mercy for their lives.

Just with these first two benefits for fearing God, it is enough to drive you to your knees and humbly begin a genuine pursuit of learning and growing in your fear of God! Yet let us move on to the third point.

3. Fearing God provides protection over our life and not fearing God diminishes the protection of God over our life.

Consider these scriptures:

> *Proverbs 14:26: "In the fear of the Lord there is strong confidence, And His children will have a place of refuge."*

> *Psalms 34:7: "The angel of the Lord encamps all around those who fear Him, And delivers them."*

> *Psalms 33:18-19: " 18 Behold, the eye of the Lord is on those who fear Him, On those who hope in His mercy, 19 To deliver their soul from death, And to keep them alive in famine."*

Psalms 115:11: "*You who fear the Lord, trust in the Lord; He is their help and their shield.*"

Matthew 10:16-28: "*16 "Behold, I send you out as sheep in the midst of wolves. Therefore be wise as serpents and harmless as doves. 17 But beware of men, for they will deliver you up to councils and scourge you in their synagogues. 18 You will be brought before governors and kings for My sake, as a testimony to them and to the Gentiles. 19 But when they deliver you up, do not worry about how or what you should speak. For it will be given to you in that hour what you should speak; 20 for it is not you who speak, but the Spirit of your Father who speaks in you. 21 Now brother will deliver up brother to death, and a father his child; and children will rise up against parents and cause them to be put to death. 22 And you will be hated by all for My name's sake. But he who endures to the end will be saved. 23 When they persecute you in this city, flee to another. For assuredly, I say to you, you will not have gone through the cities of Israel before the Son of Man comes. 24 A disciple is not above his teacher, nor a servant above his master. 25 It is enough for a disciple that he be like his teacher, and a servant like his master. If they have called the master of the house Beelzebub, how much more will they call those of his household! 26 Therefore do not fear them. For there is nothing covered that will not be revealed, and hidden that will not be known. 27 "Whatever I tell you in the dark, speak in the light; and what you hear in the ear, preach on the housetops. 28 And do not fear those who kill the body but cannot kill the soul. But rather fear Him who is able to destroy both soul and body in hell."*

There is no doubt the Lord provides protection for those who fear Him. We can see that clearly in some of the verses above. We must be careful not to take this idea of protection too far in saying that nothing negative will ever happen to those who fear God. The long passage from Matthew provides some balance and understanding to this matter.

It is important as with every Biblical doctrine to reach for the balanced truth. Our current world is notorious in taking Biblical truth and pushing it too far and creating an imbalanced version of it. A simple good example of this is the verse that says, "Whatever you ask in Jesus name you will have it." I have known way too many preachers and believers who have believed that anything and I mean anything you ask for in Jesus' name will be given to you, unless you "don't have enough faith, or have unconfessed sin in your life!" Geesh, so much garbage. John tells us in his first epistle that we have to ask according to His will to receive anything, His will, not our wants and desires! I am sure you get my point here.

The same thoughts about balance must be applied here too. The best way to consider all of this is to view these truths from the perspective of eternity. Afterall, we are going to live forever, and this life is simply a drop of water in the ocean of "forever." We know we will face persecution and difficulty living as a believer, but we should not face difficulty without the fear of God! Oh no, that would be a critical mistake on our part. We need all the protection we can get from the Lord and those who walk in the fear of God everyday can count on it!

4. Fearing God releases the Holy Spirit's work of the sanctifying process of our salvation. Little or no fear of God stalls or even stops the Holy Spirit's work of the sanctifying process of our salvation.

Consider these scriptures:

> *Psalms 85:9: "Surely His salvation is near to those who fear Him, That glory may dwell in our land."*

> *1 Peter 1:1-2: "__1__ Peter, an apostle of Jesus Christ, To the pilgrims of the Dispersion in Pontus, Galatia, Cappadocia, Asia, and Bithynia, __2__ elect according to the foreknowledge of God the Father, in sanctification of the Spirit, for obedience and sprinkling of the blood of Jesus Christ: Grace to you and peace be multiplied."*

> *Romans 12:1-2: "__1__ I beseech you therefore, brethren, by the mercies of God, that you present your bodies*

*a living sacrifice, holy, acceptable to God, which is your reasonable service. **2** And do not be conformed to this world, but be transformed by the renewing of your mind, that you may prove what is that good and acceptable and perfect will of God."*

*Philippians 2:12-13: "**12** Therefore, my beloved, as you have always obeyed, not as in my presence only, but now much more in my absence, work out your own salvation with fear and trembling;**13** for it is God who works in you both to will and to do for His good pleasure."*

This point may not be as easy to see and understand as the other points thus far, but I will try my best to explain. Considering the theology of the doctrine of salvation (as we have discussed earlier), we understand there are three aspects to what we label "salvation." One of those aspects is *justification* that focuses on the past experience of being born-again where our sins are forgiven and the penalty for sin (eternal separation from God) is removed. Another aspect is labeled *glorification* that focuses on the future whereby the actual presence of sin is removed, and we will be glorified with new bodies that will last forever in the presence of God. The third aspect is in reference to the present and is labeled *sanctification*. This present idea of salvation is all about the work of the Holy Spirit and how He is removing the power of sin over our lives. There is no way that man by himself can really overcome sin and its power over him apart from the supernatural power of the Holy Spirit doing the work. As we walk in surrender to the Lord and the fear of God, the Holy Spirit has the freedom to operate in our lives doing this work of *sanctification*.

Understanding this special work of the Holy Spirit in the lives of believers, you can see the critical place that the fear of God holds in the big picture here. In the first verse above, the "salvation that is near" is in reference to this aspect of *sanctification*, the work of the Holy Spirit. The "glory" dwelling in the land of course is about believers who because of the fear of God have this special work occurring in their lives thus resulting in God's glory in them being in the land.

The passages in 1 Peter, Romans, and Philippians are in reference to this work of the Spirit also. "Working out your own salvation with fear and trembling," is about living in the fear of God and in your surrender to the Lord, He is accomplishing this work of *sanctification*. Verse 13 in Philippians clearly states that it is God who is doing the work, not you!

Hopefully by now, you fully understand how incredibly important the work of the Holy Spirit is with regard to our salvation. You can see with little or no fear of God, this work of the Spirit is hindered, possibly even halted because God will not force anything on us against our will. The awful results are believers constantly being overwhelmed by sin in their lives. The power of sin seems to always be winning and bringing such heartaches and sorrow. In addition, believers do not grow in their faith and walk with

Jesus and the signs and expressions of immaturity seem to always be present.

The bottom line is to seek to fear God on a regular daily basis along with working hard to grow in your level of the fear of God. It will release the work of the Holy Spirit and growth and maturity will happen. Praise the Lord, fear God daily!

5. Fearing God is a weapon against sin. Little or no fear of God is an invitation and a pathway to sinful behavior.

Consider these scriptures:

Exodus 20:20: "And Moses said to the people, "Do not fear; for God has come to test you, and that His fear may be before you, so that you may not sin."

Proverbs 16:6: "In mercy and truth Atonement is provided for iniquity; And by the fear of the Lord one departs from evil."

2 Corinthians 7:1: "Therefore, having these promises, beloved, let us cleanse ourselves from all filthiness of the flesh and spirit, perfecting holiness in the fear of God."

> *1 Peter 1:17: "And if you call on the Father, who without partiality judges according to each one's work, conduct yourselves throughout the time of your stay here in fear;"*

> *Proverbs 1:24-31: "**24** Because I have called and you refused, I have stretched out my hand and no one regarded, **25** Because you disdained all my counsel, And would have none of my rebuke, **26** I also will laugh at your calamity; I will mock when your terror comes, **27** When your terror comes like a storm, And your destruction comes like a whirlwind, When distress and anguish come upon you. **28** "Then they will call on me, but I will not answer; They will seek me diligently, but they will not find me. **29** Because they hated knowledge And did not choose the fear of the Lord, **30** They would have none of my counsel And despised my every rebuke. **31** Therefore they shall eat the fruit of their own way, And be filled to the full with their own fancies."*

Obviously just a quick reading of these scriptures provides the clear picture of this point. I'm not sure if anyone else has ever considered the fear of God as a weapon against sin. These scriptures paint a beautiful picture of just how powerful the fear of God is over sin, and not only over sin itself, but fearing God provides the power to "depart from evil." Now that is power! (Please realize that this is releasing the work of the Holy Spirit.)

I have given up counting how Christians through the years have been trying to win the battle against evil and sin. Of the many "tools" available to us in order to walk in victory, fearing God is by far a huge weapon to use.

In 2 Corinthians 7:1, "perfecting holiness" is all about dealing with sin in our life; not so much to make us perfect, but to provide assurance of victory on a daily basis. This is yet another reason to shout Hallelujah and give praise to the Lord! The verb here is in the present tense which indicates the continual action of the verb and can be seen as "the action improving and getting better at it."

The verse in 1 Peter 1:17, we see an interesting verb, "conduct." This verb is in the aorist tense (indicates pin point action) and means to overthrow. What are we to overthrow? We are to overthrow ourselves, a reference to overthrowing the sinful nature. Because of the passive voice of the verb, the indication is that someone other than ourselves is doing the action… God is!!! On our behalf! We understand our accountability to the Lord, so we call out to Him for help… help me Holy Spirit!!! Wow, fearing God is such a powerful weapon against sin assisting us in our walk-in victory in Christ!

Now, think with me regarding having little or no fear of God. The opposite results will be true. The pathway to a sinful lifestyle and having little or no power over it is a constant nightmare. The only genuine remedy is to begin living in the fear of God and growing in that!

I hope it has dawned on you by now that how we have examined the fear of God, what begins to appear is just how every problem that Christians face in life are the direct results of little or no fear of God. This is a huge revelation for me and others who have walked down this avenue. Surely, we all need a big wake-up call-in relation to this and to shout from the roof-tops… "FEAR GOD!!! It is the solution to all of our problems and the sure road to a successful and victorious Christian life! So, let's move on to the next benefit.

6. Fearing God provides assurance that God hears us and remembers us. Not fearing God gives no assurance that God hears us at all.

Consider these scriptures:

> *Nehemiah 1:11: "O Lord, I pray, please let Your ear be attentive to the prayer of Your servant, and to the prayer of Your servants who desire to fear Your name;"*

> *Proverbs 15:29: "The Lord is far from the wicked, But He hears the prayer of the righteous."*

> *Proverbs 28:9: "One who turns away his ear from hearing the law, Even his prayer is an abomination."*

> *Psalms 66:18: "If I regard iniquity in my heart, The Lord will not hear."*

Psalms 145:19: "*He will fulfill the desire of those who fear Him; He also will hear their cry and save them.*"

Isaiah 1:15: "*When you spread out your hands, I will hide My eyes from you; Even though you make many prayers, I will not hear. Your hands are full of blood.*"

Isaiah 59:2: "*But your iniquities have separated you from your God; And your sins have hidden His face from you, so that He will not hear.*"

Micah 3:4: "*Then they will cry to the Lord, But He will not hear them; He will even hide His face from them at that time, because they have been evil in their deeds.*"

Malachi 3:16: "*Then those who feared the Lord spoke to one another, And the Lord listened and heard them; So, a book of remembrance was written before Him For those who fear the Lord And who meditate on His name.*"

John 9:31: "*Now we know that God does not hear sinners; but if anyone is a worshiper of God and does His will, He hears him.*"

1 Peter 3:12: "*For the eyes of the Lord are on the righteous, And His ears are open to their prayers; But the face of the Lord is against those who do evil.*"

This specific benefit and/or consequence are often debated in some Christian circles. There seems to be the sense that communicating God does not hear some people, is a culturally unacceptable matter. I have even heard a couple of leaders clearly say that "holding this position is negative and not keeping with a loving God. God hears all prayers from all people."

I do have to say in defense, after writing the book on loving people like Jesus loves us called, "The Forgotten Commandment," I do have a good idea of our loving God. But please understand that a "loving God" does not accept or tolerate sin left unresolved in a person's life, or a group or denomination. In addition, God surely hears the prayer of repentance and calling out to Him for salvation and forgiveness… that is without question. But the everyday prayers of people who have little or no fear of God following their own selfish and sinful lifestyles… well, the above scriptures speak for themselves.

I don't know about you, but my life is filled with various challenges, disappointments, burdens, and etc.; you know, a life in need of supernatural help on a daily basis. I really don't know anyone who isn't in the same place. If someone doesn't feel the need for divine assistance at this moment, just wait awhile and see what life brings. To have the confidence and assurance that God "hears" is such a comforting thought. Please understand that in all of these verses the matter of God "hearing" is so much more than verbal sounds heard by God. For God to "hear" means that He really understands the depth and meaning of our cries to Him. His love and concern move Him in responding, maybe not in the way we would like but those who fear Him know that God is in charge and has our best interests in His heart at all times. Praise the Lord for His ear tuned to our hearts and voices! Those who fear God can be assured of this, every day, every hour, and every minute!

If you have little or no fear of God, the opposite is true. These verses speak to this loud and clear. Make no mistake and don't be beguiled by current teachers who would have you believe that God "hears" everyone no matter what. They have either not read these scriptures or they are speaking for the Devil to confuse and deceive. From the Old Testament through the New Testament, this truth stands clear! So, fear God!!!

7. Fearing God opens a door so the Lord can confide in us, sharing many intimate things about His covenant with us. Not fearing God leads us to miss these special secrets.

Consider this scripture:

> Psalm 25:14: "The secret of the Lord is with those who fear Him, And He will show them His covenant."

This is such a powerful verse of scripture that states clearly about the Lord intimately confiding in us. The Hebrew word for "secret" is a word that means a confidential discussion with a close and personal friend. This is not about God having certain "secrets" that He keeps from most people and only shares them with some. The emphasis is on the close intimacy of what is shared. In other words, God is yearning to have close, personal, and intimate time with each and every one of us, to share His heart, His will, and His direction for our lives. He is able to bring comfort, encouragement, and inspiration to us, but only to those who fear Him.

The Hebrew word for "show" brings even more emphasis to this idea. This word means to show in such a way that it will teach that you can learn and know with your heart and mind His covenant, His promises, and blessings for us! What a great benefit for us who fear God!

Unfortunately, those who have little, or no fear of God miss most of this. They might feel in the dark or somehow out of touch with God. They might even think that those who are always talking about what they are hearing from the Lord are phonies or just caught up in their own delusion. The fact of the matter is that those with little or no fear of God are the ones caught up in their own selfish thinking and are disconnected with God; never really experiencing any true and genuine intimacy with Him. What a shame! My advice to move out of this consequence… fear God!!!

8. Fearing God brings delight to the Lord. Little or no fear of God breaks God's heart.

Consider these scriptures:

Psalm 147:11a: "The Lord takes pleasure in those who fear Him,"

Ephesians 4:30: "And do not grieve the Holy Spirit of God, by whom you were sealed for the day of redemption."

Genesis 6:5-6: "**5** Then the Lord saw that the wickedness of man was great in the earth, and that every intent of the thoughts of his heart was only evil continually. **6** And the Lord was sorry that He had made man on the earth, and He was grieved in His heart.

If there is anyone that I want to bring joy and pleasure to, it's God. I believe for the most part, all true believers desire the same thing. In fact, I have seen so many trying to do so many things that they think God will derive joy from, that it has frustrated their lives. The simple truth of the matter is that God derives joy and pleasure from those who fear Him. The word "take" here in Psalm 147 can easily be translated "receives." Fearing God brings delight to God on a constant basis. Unfortunately, the opposite is true also.

The two passages listed above although they do not use the words, "little or no fear of God," obviously are describing individuals who have little or no fear of God. The definitions provided in this book make this a clear reality. What we need to see is the consequence for living without the fear of God. In both passages, the consequence is clear, it "grieves" the heart of God. Paul warns us not to "grieve" God. The passage in Genesis is quite shocking in nature. This is where God is grieved so deeply in His heart because almost everyone on earth is without any fear of Him and they are full of wickedness. The destruction by flood is next to come.

What I would like to focus on is the Hebrew word found here translated "grieved." The Hebrew word used to describe God's sorrow in this passage is "nacham." It means to "draw the breath forcibly." It is a deep sigh of painful sorrow. Have you ever hurt so bad inside that you could hardly get your breath? That is the kind of sorrow God is experiencing here. It's as if God is saying "Oooh, Oooh" such grief that is expressed only in groans because it is beyond words.

The question we have to ask ourselves is "do we want to bring delight to God's heart, or do we want to break His heart?" Fear God! This is what makes the difference!

9. Fearing God helps us to easily hear God and be divinely instructed. Not fearing God leads us to easily miss God speaking or being divinely instructed.

Consider these scriptures:

*Proverbs 1:20-33: "**20** Wisdom calls aloud outside; She raises her voice in the open squares. **21** She cries out in the chief concourses, At the openings of the gates in the city She speaks her words: **22** "How long, you simple ones, will you love simplicity? For scorners delight in their scorning, And fools hate knowledge. **23** Turn at my rebuke; Surely I will pour out my spirit on you; I will make my words known to you. **24** Because I have called and you refused, I have stretched out my hand and no one regarded, **25** Because you disdained all my counsel, And would have none of my rebuke, **26** I also will laugh at your calamity; I will mock when your terror comes, **27** When your terror comes like a storm, And your destruction comes like a whirlwind, When distress and anguish come upon you. **28** "Then they will call on me, but I will not answer; They will seek me diligently, but they will not find me. **29** Because they hated knowledge And did not choose the fear of the Lord, **30** They would have none of my counsel And despised my every rebuke. **31** Therefore they shall eat the fruit of their own way, And be filled to the full with their own fancies. **32** For* the turning away of the simple will slay them, And the complacency of fools will destroy them; **33** But whoever listens to me will dwell safely, And will be secure, without fear of evil."

Psalms 25:12: "Who is the man that fears the Lord? Him shall He teach in the way He chooses."

Acts 9:10-18: "**10** Now there was a certain disciple at Damascus named Ananias; and to him the Lord said in a vision, "Ananias." And he said, "Here I am, Lord." **11** So the Lord said to him, "Arise and go to the street called Straight, and inquire at the house of Judas for one called Saul of Tarsus, for behold, he is praying. **12** And in a vision he has seen a man named Ananias coming in and putting his hand on him, so that he might receive his sight." **13** Then Ananias answered, "Lord, I have heard from many about this man, how much harm he has done to Your saints in Jerusalem. **14** And here he has authority from the chief priests to bind all who call on Your name." **15** But the Lord said to him, "Go, for he is a chosen vessel of Mine to bear My name before Gentiles, kings, and the children of Israel. **16** For I will show him how many things he must suffer for My name's sake." **17** And Ananias went his way and entered the house; and laying his hands on him he said, "Brother Saul, the Lord Jesus, who appeared to you on the road as you came, has sent me that you may receive your sight and be filled with the Holy Spirit." **18** *Immediately there fell from his eyes something like scales, and he received his sight at once; and he arose and was baptized."*

Acts 10:2-6: " **2** *a devout man and one who feared God with all his household, who gave alms generously to the people, and prayed to God always.* **3** *About the ninth hour of the day he saw clearly in a vision an angel of God coming in and saying to him, "Cornelius!"* **4** *And when he observed him, he was afraid, and said, "What is it, lord?" So he said to him, "Your prayers and your alms have come up for a memorial before God.* **5** *Now send men to Joppa, and send for Simon whose surname is Peter.* **6** *He is lodging with Simon, a tanner, whose house is by the sea. He will tell you what you must do."*

Acts 10:22: "*And they said, "Cornelius the centurion, a just man, one who fears God and has a good reputation among all the nation of the Jews, was divinely instructed by a holy angel to summon you to his house, and to hear words from you."*

John 10:27: "*My sheep hear My voice, and I know them, and they follow Me."*

There is considerable scripture listed here. There could be so many other passages added to this brief list. The Bible is full of stories and passages where God is speaking and directing His followers. Hearing God is an essential discipline of the Christian life. It really is extremely important as John 10:27 indicates. But this matter of hearing God is reported by so many believers to be an exceedingly difficult experience to have, especially on a regular basis. The benefit of fearing God simply makes it easier to hear God and be divinely directed and instructed by Him.

Could it be that the reason hearing God is such a difficulty among Christians is because they have little or no fear of God? As we reconsider the seven features of fearing God, it is easy to see why this particular benefit surfaces so clearly. The passage in Proverbs 1 indicates that the lack of the fear of God has contributed to their problem of not hearing God and not being able to be clearly directed by God, leading to judgment!

The passage in Acts 9 regarding Ananias is quite interesting. The passage doesn't specifically report that Ananias was a man who feared God but consider the situation. The Lord is directing Ananias to go to Saul of Tarsus and essentially share the gospel of Jesus Christ with him. Saul was hunting down people who claimed to be Christians to persecute them, throw them into jail, and confiscate their possessions. He was feared among everyone who was a follower of Jesus. It would take a greater fear of God to overcome the fear of Saul to perform and obey what Ananias was told by God. As the passage records, Ananias obeyed God without question. Obviously, he feared God more than most!

As a believer, I strongly desire to hear the Lord and to hear Him daily. I want to obey Him and clearly know He has spoken and directed me. I believe this is the heart of every genuine Christian. This particular benefit as discussed urges me to want to grow in my fear of God even more. How about you?

10. Fearing God places us in a position to be appointed and entrusted by God to special assignments and positions. Little or no fear of God causes us to miss or misunderstand divine appointments and special assignments from God.

Consider these scriptures:

> Nehemiah 7:1-2: " *__1__ Then it was, when the wall was built and I had hung the doors, when the gatekeepers, the singers, and the Levites had been appointed, __2__ that I gave the charge of Jerusalem to my brother Hanani, and Hananiah the leader of the citadel, for he was a faithful man and feared God more than many."*

> Exodus 18:21-22a: " *__21__ Moreover you shall select from all the people able men, such as fear God, men of truth, hating covetousness; and place such over them to be rulers of thousands, rulers of hundreds,*

rulers of fifties, and rulers of tens. **22** *And let them judge the people at all times."*

Psalm 60:4:" You have given a banner to those who fear You, That it may be displayed because of the truth. Selah"

Acts 6:3-7:" **3** *Therefore, brethren, seek out from among you seven men of good reputation, full of the Holy Spirit and wisdom, whom we may appoint over this business;* **4** *but we will give ourselves continually to prayer and to the ministry of the word."* **5** *And the saying pleased the whole multitude. And they chose Stephen, a man full of faith and the Holy Spirit, and Philip, Prochorus, Nicanor, Timon, Parmenas, and Nicolas, a proselyte from Antioch,* **6** *whom they set before the apostles; and when they had prayed, they laid hands on them.* **7** *Then the word of God spread, and the number of the disciples multiplied greatly in Jerusalem, and a great many of the priests were obedient to the faith."*

Acts 9:10-18:" **10** *Now there was a certain disciple at Damascus named Ananias; and to him the Lord said in a vision, "Ananias." And he said, "Here I am, Lord."* **11** *So the Lord said to him, "Arise and go to the street called Straight, and inquire at the house of Judas for one called Saul of Tarsus, for behold, he is praying.* **12** *And in a vision he has seen a man named Ananias* *coming in and putting his hand on him, so that he might receive his sight." **13** Then Ananias answered, "Lord, I have heard from many about this man, how much harm he has done to Your saints in Jerusalem. **14** And here he has authority from the chief priests to bind all who call on Your name." **15** But the Lord said to him, "Go, for he is a chosen vessel of Mine to bear My name before Gentiles, kings, and the children of Israel. **16** For I will show him how many things he must suffer for My name's sake." **17** And Ananias went his way and entered the house; and laying his hands on him he said, "Brother Saul, the Lord Jesus, who appeared to you on the road as you came, has sent me that you may receive your sight and be filled with the Holy Spirit." **18** Immediately there fell from his eyes something like scales, and he received his sight at once; and he arose and was baptized."*

From the beginning of time, God has been speaking, directing, and appointing individuals and nations to special assignments. God is able to use anyone for His purposes. He has even used the Devil and many wicked and evil rulers to accomplish His purposes. But I do have to add that the Devil and these evil rulers had no clue what was going on. They not only misunderstood these assignments from God, but they also had no idea to even gain an ounce of understanding.

Now, with that being said, let's journey deeper into this truth particularly with regard to the people of God.

The above scriptures are only a sample from both the Old and New Testaments of the numerous occurrences of God revealing and directing his chosen servants by divine appointments and special assignments. These examples especially from the Old Testament are quite specific in nature indicating that it was the fear of God that established the appointments and assignments.

When we are living and growing in the fear of God, it places us in positions to not only hear the Lord but also to be selected for special opportunities. I believe that every believer who is serious about their walk and faith in the Lord has desires in their hearts to be used of the Lord in many wonderful ways. I have lost count of the Christians that have come to me with serious questions about how to really hear God and know for sure His direction for their lives. I am sorry to say that for many years I did not have clear definitive answers for them, but now I do! Fear God! Live daily in the fear of God and continually be seeking to grow in your fear of God. Those who follow this admonition will discover the wonderful and glorious direction of the Lord and experience with certainty God's appointment and trust for divine and special assignments from Him.

It is sad to say that too many believers with little or no fear of God are missing or misunderstanding God's appointments and assignments in their lives. I am afraid to say how many people have made poor and wrong decisions maybe just out of their own selfish desires to be in ministry or leadership roles in some manner and now are conducting their lives without God's divine choice and anointing, they are only serving themselves. The issue is that some are using worldly techniques and methods and appear to be quite successful, but on the inside, they are full of "dead man's bones." Jesus addressed numerous leaders in His own day that fit into this category. Don't think for a moment that things are any different today. Because so many Christians have little or no fear of God and have little understanding of how to develop the fear of God, this matter is much more widespread than we could ever realize! May God have mercy on us… and lead us to making the fear of God a serious priority in our lives!

11. Fearing God is the basis and the avenue for genuine spiritual wisdom and knowledge. Little or no fear of God will cause a lack of spiritual wisdom and knowledge.

Consider these scriptures:

Proverbs 1:7: "*The fear of the Lord is the beginning of knowledge, But fools despise wisdom and instruction.*"

Proverbs 9:10: "*The fear of the Lord is the beginning of wisdom, And the knowledge of the Holy One is understanding.*"

When it comes to the fear of God, these two verses may be the most well known in the Bible. I'm sure we have all quoted them on multiple occasions for various reasons. It is worthwhile to take a few minutes to intentionally consider what they are communicating to us.

The word used in both verses, "beginning," actually means "what comes first." Simple as that sounds it is the main reason for this book and the main reason why Christians have all the problems they do. Fearing God must be first in our life. This means that it must be a priority. This is not something that you put on your list to do sometime in your life. It is not something that you add to whatever you are doing already. The emphasis here is to stop everything else and put fearing God first! The importance of fearing God rises to the top of the list. Oh, what a difference life would be for us and for our churches; just think about it for a minute. With everything we have already communicated, that is enough to lead us to fall on our knees in repentance and seek God's forgiveness and put us on the main track of making and keeping fearing God first!

We can see clearly from these verses that the fear of God is the beginning of spiritual knowledge and wisdom. Is it possible that the lack of the fear of God is what is causing such spiritual ignorance in Christian's lives today? I am reminded of the four dangerous positions believers can be in today as I mentioned in the start of this chapter. Please realize that ignorance is the precursor of easily being deceived by the enemy of our souls! This might be the reason why so many church people have been led astray by "doctrines of demons" and ending up in lifeless churches, dangerous cults of deception, or just disillusioned and no longer living a genuine Christian life out of touch with God's word, God's people, and isolated alone. Again, my only advice is to fear God, live daily fearing God and grow in your fear of God!

12. Fearing God is how rewards are built up in heaven. Little or no fear of God is how rewards are lost for heaven and the degrees of torment are determined in hell

Consider these scriptures:

> *Revelation 11:18: "The nations were angry, and Your wrath has come, And the time of the dead, that they should be judged, And that You should reward Your servants the prophets and the saints, And those who fear Your name, small and great, And should destroy those who destroy the earth."*

> *Revelation 20:12-15: "__12__ And I saw the dead, small and great, standing before God, and books were opened. And another book was opened, which is the Book of Life. And the dead were judged according to their works, by the things which were written in the books. __13__ The sea gave up the dead who were in it, and Death and Hades delivered up the dead who were*

in them. And they were judged, each one according to his works. **14** Then Death and Hades were cast into the lake of fire. This is the second death. **15** And anyone not found written in the Book of Life was cast into the lake of fire."

Matthew 5:12: "Rejoice and be exceedingly glad, for great is your reward in heaven, for so they persecuted the prophets who were before you.

Matthew 10:14-15: "**14** And whoever will not receive you nor hear your words, when you depart from that house or city, shake off the dust from your feet. **15** Assuredly, I say to you, it will be more tolerable for the land of Sodom and Gomorrah in the day of judgment than for that city!"

Matthew 16:27: "For the Son of Man will come in the glory of His Father with His angels, and then He will reward each according to his works."
Matthew 23:14: "Woe to you, scribes and Pharisees, hypocrites! For you devour widows' houses, and for a pretense make long prayers. Therefore you will receive greater condemnation."

1 Corinthians 3:11-17: "**11** For no other foundation can anyone lay than that which is laid, which is Jesus Christ. **12** Now if anyone builds on this foundation with gold, silver, precious stones, wood, hay, straw,

***13** each one's work will become clear; for the Day will declare it, because it will be revealed by fire; and the fire will test each one's work, of what sort it is. **14** If anyone's work which he has built on it endures, he will receive a reward. **15** If anyone's work is burned, he will suffer loss; but he himself will be saved, yet so as through fire. **16** Do you not know that you are the temple of God and that the Spirit of God dwells in you? **17** If anyone defiles the temple of God, God will destroy him. For the temple of God is holy, which temple you are."*

2 Corinthians 5:8-11: *"**8** We are confident, yes, well pleased rather to be absent from the body and to be present with the Lord. **9** Therefore we make it our aim, whether present or absent, to be well pleasing to Him. **10** For we must all appear before the judgment seat of Christ, that each one may receive the things done in the body, according to what he has done, whether good or bad. **11** Knowing, therefore, the terror of the Lord, we persuade men; but we are well known to God, and I also trust are well known in your consciences."*

Philippians 2:12: "Therefore, my beloved, as you have always obeyed, not as in my presence only, but now much more in my absence, work out your own salvation with fear and trembling;"

James 3:1: "My brethren, let not many of you become teachers, knowing that we shall receive a stricter judgment."

*2 Peter 2:20-22: "**20** For if, after they have escaped the pollutions of the world through the knowledge of the Lord and Savior Jesus Christ, they are again entangled in them and overcome, the latter end is worse for them than the beginning. **21** For it would have been better for them not to have known the way of righteousness, than having known it, to turn from the holy commandment delivered to them. **22** But it has happened to them according to the true proverb: "A dog returns to his own vomit," and, "a sow, having washed, to her wallowing in the mire."*

While sitting in the office of the senior pastor of a large church where I was an associate pastor, I was shocked by a conversation we shared together. It was related to what happens to believers after death and if there would be a judgment of any sort. The pastor told me directly that a Christian is fully forgiven of all sins, and everyone would be equal in heaven and there would be absolutely no judgment at all for believers. I was shocked and totally disagreed with him. All these listed scriptures provide unmistakable evidence that he was wrong. He would not listen to any biblical scripture or spiritual reasoning. Unfortunately, he was involved in several scandalous activities that finally caught up with him. He was fired and to this day he no longer is in any ministerial role and is in the world of business continually engaging in questionable activities. I'm sure you figured that out from the beginning of the story. What is really saddening is that this story has been and is continually being repeated over and over again by more religious leaders than we could dare imagine! You already know the answer to the question "why?" Little or no fear of God!

The fear of God is all about being accountable to the Lord for the way we live. Although as a true believer in Jesus Christ I will not go to Hell for my sins, I realize that I will still be standing before the Lord in judgment and may lose any and all rewards for eternity. I can't imagine what that really means and to tell you the truth, I don't want to find out! What I want is to fear God every day and to grow in that fear as much as I can, and I hope you will join me with a whole heart!

I have quoted all of these scriptures in order to prove my point. There are many more and as you grow in your devotion to the word of God you will discover them. What is important to grasp at this point is that through the fear of God you can be building up a host of rewards for your future in eternity. In fact, it is the very fear of God that motivates us, leads us, and directs us to build these rewards. As Paul tells us in Philippians 2:12, we are to be working out our salvation in the fear of God. It is important and a priority as we have already discussed.

Conclusion

I realize that I can be a little repetitive and it is intentional. I want to drive home the incredible importance of fearing God. As I began this chapter with some important insights, I want to reiterate those thoughts once again. I believe it's important to once again consider the four dangerous positions that believers can fall into in these days of evil that are contributing to the lack of the fear of God and resulting in the multitude of problems Christians face today:

- **Ignorance – You just don't know about something important.**
- **Distracted – You might know about something important but other things are more of a priority to you.**
- **Rebellion – You may know or not know about something important, but you just don't care or want anything to do with it.**
- **Deceived – You just know the wrong or partial information about something important.**

Either one of these can be a dangerous position. The fourth one as noted before, is a place that too many Christian leaders and teachers are in. After so many years as a leader myself, traveling around the world in ministry, I see the reality of this everywhere. Please be aware and seriously consider, lest you get stuck in one of these positions!

We spend time, effort, and prayer in building the fear of the Lord in our lives through focusing on the seven features. It wouldn't hurt to rehearse them again over in our mind. As these features of the fear of God grow and are built up in our lives, we have naturally flowing out of our lives, the characteristics discussed in the last chapter and the benefits discussed in this chapter. If these characteristics and benefits are weak or lacking, we need to spend more time building these features rather than getting sidetracked trying to work on the characteristics and benefits.

Now, once we have these seven features growing and stable in our lives the results will be the benefits in a person's life that fears the Lord more than most. Obviously, the opposite consequences will be reality for those who have little or no fear of God. Hopefully, our focus in discussing these twelve clear benefits or consequences of fearing or not fearing God have stimulated your heart to make fearing God a priority in your life!

CHAPTER FIVE:

What Causes Us to Lose the Fear of The Lord?

THERE ARE SO MANY CAUSES that lead to losing the fear of God in our lives. In this chapter we will consider twelve of them. Just don't be fooled into thinking that these twelve are all that there are just like in the other chapters of this book. It is my understanding and belief that as we continue to grow in our devotion to the Word of God (one of the seven features of the fear of God), we will discover numerous other causes. The Holy Spirit is committed to helping us to grow in all areas of our Christian life. He will certainly point out additional causes that might be impacting your life as well as others. What I am trying to say is that this list is not exhaustive, but these twelve will present a huge challenge to our hearts to be on guard!

In addition, please understand why I have placed so many scriptures with each point as with other chapters. What I have to say is nowhere near as important as to what God's word has to say. In this full study of the fear of God, I want you to see how prevalent and important it is in scripture. This is what has raised so much concern in my heart related to the lack of solid biblical teaching about the fear of God and the absolute mess Christians are in today not realizing what is the real problem! As we have carefully and fully made the point of the importance of the fear of God, now let's consider how we can begin losing this precious biblical truth. I am sure that many of these will come as no surprise. So, let us begin:

1. The development of pride and the lack of humility

Consider these scriptures:

> *Jeremiah 44:7-10: "7 Now therefore, thus says the Lord, the God of hosts, the God of Israel: 'Why do you commit this great evil against yourselves, to cut off from you man and woman, child and infant, out of Judah, leaving none to remain, 8 in that you provoke Me to wrath with the works of your hands, burning incense to other gods in the land of Egypt where you*

have gone to dwell, that you may cut yourselves off and be a curse and a reproach among all the nations of the earth? **9** Have you forgotten the wickedness of your fathers, the wickedness of the kings of Judah, the wickedness of their wives, your own wickedness, and the wickedness of your wives, which they ommitted in the land of Judah and in the streets of Jerusalem? **10** They have not been humbled, to this day, nor have they feared; they have not walked in My law or in My statutes that I set before you and your fathers.'"

James 4:6: "But He gives more grace. Therefore He says: "God resists the proud, But gives grace to the humble."

Proverbs 11:2: "When pride comes, then comes shame; But with the humble is wisdom."

(Lucifer's fall) Ezekiel 28:11-19: "**11** Moreover the word of the Lord came to me, saying, **12** "Son of man, take up a lamentation for the king of Tyre, and say to him, 'Thus says the Lord God: "You were the seal of perfection, Full of wisdom and perfect in beauty. **13** You were in Eden, the garden of God; Every precious stone was your covering: The sardius, topaz, and diamond, Beryl, onyx, and jasper, Sapphire, turquoise, and emerald with gold. The workmanship of your timbrels and pipes Was prepared for you on the day you were created. **14** "You were the anointed cherub who covers; I established you; You were on the holy mountain of God; You walked back and forth in the midst of fiery stones. **15** You were perfect in your ways from the day you were created, Till iniquity was found in you. **16** "By the abundance of your trading You became filled with violence within, And you sinned; Therefore I cast you as a profane thing Out of the mountain of God; And I destroyed you, O covering cherub, From the midst of the fiery stones. **17** "Your heart was lifted up because of your beauty; You corrupted your wisdom for the sake of your splendor; I cast you to the ground, I laid you before kings, That they might gaze at you.

18 "You defiled your sanctuaries By the multitude of your iniquities, By the iniquity of your trading; Therefore I brought fire from your midst; It devoured you, And I turned you to ashes upon the earth In the sight of all who saw you.

19 All who knew you among the peoples are astonished at you; You have become a horror, And shall be no more forever."

(Lucifer's fall) Isaiah 14:12-17: "**12** "How you are fallen from heaven, O Lucifer, son of the morning! How you are cut down to the ground, You who weakened the nations! **13** For you have said in your heart: 'I will ascend into heaven, I will exalt my throne above *the stars of God; I will also sit on the mount of the congregation On the farthest sides of the north;* **14** *I will ascend above the heights of the clouds, I will be like the Most High.'* **15** *Yet you shall be brought down to Sheol, To the lowest depths of the Pit.* **16** *"Those who see you will gaze at you, And consider you, saying: 'Is this the man who made the earth tremble, Who shook kingdoms,* **17** *Who made the world as a wilderness And destroyed its cities, Who did not open the house of his prisoners?'"*

The seventh feature of the fear of God is all about humility and seeking daily to crucify our pride. It almost goes without saying that allowing pride to grow in our mind and heart would deteriorate our fear of God. Many theologians have indicated that pride is the deadliest sin of all because it blinds you from realizing its presence and growth.

There are so many other scriptures that could be quoted here, but these will do for bringing the point to bear. In Jeremiah 44:10, the verse summarizes the sins of the people and the reason for pending judgment from God, no humility… no fear of God. The fear of God brings us into an intimate relationship with the Lord. It's going to be hard to be intimate when God resists the proud as James expresses how God feels about pride.

The two longer passages have long been considered by most theologians as descriptions of the Devil as the fallen angel Lucifer. They describe Lucifer as well as explain why he fell from such a high level of position among the angels.

To boil his fall down to one word is to say pride entered his heart and caused the fall. Some have even said that Adam and Eve's fall in sin was because of pride (to be as God). Obviously, pride and the lack of humility is a dangerous sin and leaves anyone found with it in a bad place. We can easily summarize that the development of pride and the lack of humility will cause us to lose the fear of God.

2. Negative responses to life's circumstances

Consider these scriptures:

*Matthew 27:3-5: "**3** Then Judas, His betrayer, seeing that He had been condemned, was remorseful and brought back the thirty pieces of silver to the chief priests and elders, **4** saying, "I have sinned by betraying innocent blood." And they said, "What is that to us? You see to it!" **5** Then he threw down the pieces of silver in the temple and departed, and went and hanged himself."*

*1 Corinthians 10:1-11: "**1** Moreover, brethren, I do not want you to be unaware that all our fathers were under the cloud, all passed through the sea, **2** all were baptized into Moses in the cloud and in the sea, **3** all ate the same spiritual food, **4** and all drank the same spiritual drink. For they drank of that spiritual Rock that followed them, and that Rock was Christ. **5** But* with most of them God was not well pleased, for their bodies were scattered in the wilderness. **6** Now these things became our examples, to the intent that we should not lust after evil things as they also lusted. **7** And do not become idolaters as were some of them. As it is written, "The people sat down to eat and drink, and rose up to play." **8** Nor let us commit sexual immorality, as some of them did, and in one day twenty-three thousand fell; **9** nor let us tempt Christ, as some of them also tempted, and were destroyed by serpents; **10** nor complain, as some of them also complained, and were destroyed by the destroyer. **11** Now all these things happened to them as examples, and they were written for our admonition, upon whom the ends of the ages have come."

2 Corinthians 4:16-18: "**16** Therefore we do not lose heart. Even though our outward man is perishing, yet the inward man is being renewed day by day. **17** For our light affliction, which is but for a moment, is working for us a far more exceeding and eternal weight of glory, **18** while we do not look at the things which are seen, but at the things which are not seen. For the things which are seen are temporary, but the things which are not seen are eternal."

Romans 8:28: "And we know that all things work together for good to those who love God, to those who are the called according to His purpose."

We can be sure of this fact: troubles will come in this life. Some experience more than others, but we all have difficulties from time to time. Because we are strong believers and filled with the Holy Spirit, even living firmly in the fear of God does not provide immunity from difficult life circumstances. Just a couple of the above verses give a clear indication of this. In fact, there are verses where Jesus, Paul, Peter, and James tell us that being a good solid Christian will be the very reason for troubled life circumstances.

These troubled circumstances do not negate the teaching about the fear of God that brings blessings and protection in our lives. This also is true, but from a place of spiritual maturity, we must understand that we live in a fallen world that is filled with sin and that the free will of man provides opportunities for people to do horrible things to innocent individuals and groups. We must always seek to view this life in the sphere of eternity, not just the temporal experience we are in. God's desire to form us into the image of Christ and to glorify Himself actually requires times of testing and trials. The lessons we have learned from long-term prisoners of war who were believers, is that it's more about what is happening on the inside, in our hearts and minds rather than the outward circumstances. Humbly drawing and pressing into God's presence is absolutely necessary in order to counterbalance the difficulties of life we face.

The passages in 2 Corinthians 4 and Romans 8:28 take on a deeper meaning and provide clearer insight into what I am communicating here. When our understanding is darkened or lacking altogether, then unfortunately the response to these difficulties becomes negative!

When we have negative responses to life's circumstances, they become an avenue to begin travelling away from having the fear of God. The hurt, pain, frustration, etc. leads us to question God's presence or genuine love for us. Temptation from our enemy is always quick to throw questions about God's ability and desire for our welfare and it can become easy to start speaking outwardly what our enemy is speaking inwardly to us. Our faith is shaken, our trust in God is weakened, and our hope and confidence in God is disappearing before our very eyes. Our fear of God is being lost and the consequences will be disastrous!

This is a struggle for all of us, but we must hold firm to our fear of God. We must seek with all of our hearts to keep growing in the features of the fear of God; not forgetting the need to be filled with the Holy Spirit and surrendered to Him in order to help us in these pursuits.

3. Lack of sowing into the Kingdom of God.

Consider these scriptures:

> *Deuteronomy 14:23: "And you shall eat before the Lord your God, in the place where He chooses to make His name abide, the tithe of your grain and your new wine and your oil, of the firstborn of your*

herds and your flocks, that you may learn to fear the Lord your God always."

Proverbs 11:24: "There is one who scatters yet increases more; And there is one who withholds more than is right, But it leads to poverty."

*Malachi 6:6-12: "**6** "For I am the Lord, I do not change; Therefore you are not consumed, O sons of Jacob. **7** Yet from the days of your fathers You have gone away from My ordinances And have not kept them. Return to Me, and I will return to you," Says the Lord of hosts. "But you said, 'In what way shall we return?' **8** "Will a man rob God? Yet you have robbed Me! But you say, 'In what way have we robbed You?' In tithes and offerings. **9** You are cursed with a curse, For you have robbed Me, Even this whole nation. **10** Bring all the tithes into the storehouse, That there may be food in My house, And try Me now in this," Says the Lord of hosts, "If I will not open for you the windows of heaven And pour out for you such blessing That there will not be room enough to receive it. **11** "And I will rebuke the devourer for your sakes, So that he will not destroy the fruit of your ground, Nor shall the vine fail to bear fruit for you in the field," Says the Lord of hosts; **12** "And all nations will call you blessed, For you will be a delightful land," Says the Lord of hosts.*

Galatians 6:7-10: "**7** *Do not be deceived, God is not mocked; for whatever a man sows, that he will also reap.* **8** *For he who sows to his flesh will of the flesh reap corruption, but he who sows to the Spirit will of the Spirit reap everlasting life.* **9** *And let us not grow weary while doing good, for in due season we shall reap if we do not lose heart.* **10** *Therefore, as we have opportunity, let us do good to all, especially to those who are of the household of faith.*

No matter what your theological position is regarding the matter of tithing, the issue here is about sowing into the Kingdom of God. In the verse in Deuteronomy, we are clearly told by tithing we are able to learn the fear of God. It is interesting that the verse states "always." This Hebrew word is quite interesting because it actually means "day or daylight." We are able to derive from this that we are to learn the fear of God in the "daylight" where things can be clearly observed and understood. Trying to see and learn something in the dark can create a misinterpretation or an obscured vision of it. Learning in the light of day creates the possibility of the most accurate understanding of a particular topic.

The other verses lend credence and validity to the whole idea presented here. When there is a lack of sowing into the Kingdom of God, the focus of attention and desire is on something other than the Lord and His priorities. This provides an easy avenue away from the fear of God and leads you to a place of difficulty and even judgment from the

Lord. You could easily say that this is nothing more than the expression of selfishness bringing severe consequences now and in the future.

There is a strong admonition from the Apostle Paul in the Galatians passage focusing on this. He indicates that the spirit of deception is at work and horrible consequences are going to be reaped sooner or later. If anything, learn this: sowing joyfully and regularly into the Kingdom of God teaches the fear of God. Choose not to be a giver and the fear of God will disappear from your life!

4. Unequally yoked in relationships

Consider these scriptures:

> *Joshua 22:25:" For the Lord has made the Jordan a border between you and us, you children of Reuben and children of Gad. You have no part in the Lord." So your descendants would make our descendants cease fearing the Lord."*

> *Proverbs 12:26: "The righteous should choose his friends carefully, For the way of the wicked leads them astray."*

> *2 Corinthians 6:14-17: "__14__ Do not be unequally yoked together with unbelievers. For what fellowship has righteousness with lawlessness? And what com-*

*munion has light with darkness? **15** And what accord has Christ with Belial? Or what part has a believer with an unbeliever? **16** And what agreement has the temple of God with idols? For you are the temple of the living God. As God has said: "I will dwell in them And walk among them. I will be their God, And they shall be My people." **17** Therefore "Come out from among them And be separate, says the Lord. Do not touch what is unclean, And I will receive you."*

In the culture of today's world, the focus of struggle and arguments seems to be on matters of inappropriate sexual expressions, transgender manipulations, and general gender identity. These sinful desires and expressions are unravelling the very fabric of our culture. There should be a loud outcry and call to our culture to repent and turn to Jesus and what He has created as normal human life both biologically and psychologically. But we must not lose sight of what the scripture teaches us about unequally yoked relationships.

Unequally yoked relationships have to do with believers being connected to unbelievers in meaningful relationships. They can be in romantic and close friendship relationships, business relationships, as well as committed relationships to organizations that are clearly not Christian oriented or in line with Biblical priorities.

The verse in Joshua makes it very clear that unequally yoked relationships will cause the fear of God to cease. The verse in Proverbs gives the same indication. Paul, in the 2

Corinthians passage, is quite direct in providing the command to not be in this kind of relationship. There are no "if, ands, or buts." It is wrong because of what the results of a relationship of this kind leads to. We can see that the fear of God is at stake here and unequally yoked relationships "suck" the fear of God out of a believer's heart and mind! Much more about this matter needs to be proclaimed from the pulpits across our world and in the discipling of believers in following Christ.

5. Inappropriately dealing with sins in our life by:

- Justifying
- Minimizing
- Rationalizing
- Blame-shifting

Consider these scriptures:

> *Proverbs 1:22-31: "**22** "How long, you simple ones, will you love simplicity? For scorners delight in their scorning, And fools hate knowledge. **23** Turn at my rebuke; Surely I will pour out my spirit on you; I will make my words known to you. **24** Because I have called and you refused, I have stretched out my hand and no one regarded, **25** Because you disdained all my counsel, And would have none of my rebuke, **26** I*

also will laugh at your calamity; I will mock when your terror comes, **27** *When your terror comes like a storm, And your destruction comes like a whirlwind, When distress and anguish come upon you.* **28** *"Then they will call on me, but I will not answer; They will seek me diligently, but they will not find me.* **29** *Because they hated knowledge And did not choose the fear of the Lord,* **30** *They would have none of my counsel And despised my every rebuke.* **31** *Therefore they shall eat the fruit of their own way, And be filled to the full with their own fancies."*

*Proverbs 6:12-19: "***12** *A worthless person, a wicked man, Walks with a perverse mouth;* **13** *He winks with his eyes, He shuffles his feet, He points with his fingers;* **14** *Perversity is in his heart, He devises evil continually, He sows discord.* **15** *Therefore his calamity shall come suddenly; Suddenly he shall be broken without remedy.* **16** *These six things the Lord hates, Yes, seven are an abomination to Him:* **17** *A proud look, A lying tongue, Hands that shed innocent blood,* **18** *A heart that devises wicked plans, Feet that are swift in running to evil,* **19** *A false witness who speaks lies, And one who sows discord among brethren."*

*Romans 1:18-32: "***18** *For the wrath of God is revealed from heaven against all ungodliness and unrighteousness of men, who suppress the truth in unrighteous-*

ness, **19** because what may be known of God is manifest in them, for God has shown it to them. **20** For since the creation of the world His invisible attributes are clearly seen, being understood by the things that are made, even His eternal power and Godhead, so that they are without excuse, **21** because, although they knew God, they did not glorify Him as God, nor were thankful, but became futile in their thoughts, and their foolish hearts were darkened. **22** Professing to be wise, they became fools, **23** and changed the glory of the incorruptible God into an image made like corruptible man--and birds and four-footed animals and creeping things. **24** Therefore God also gave them up to uncleanness, in the lusts of their hearts, to dishonor their bodies among themselves, **25** who exchanged the truth of God for the lie, and worshiped and served the creature rather than the Creator, who is blessed forever. Amen. **26** For this reason God gave them up to vile passions. For even their women exchanged the natural use for what is against nature. **27** Likewise also the men, leaving the natural use of the woman, burned in their lust for one another, men with men committing what is shameful, and receiving in themselves the penalty of their error which was due. **28** And even as they did not like to retain God in their knowledge, God gave them over to a debased mind, to do those things which are not fitting; **29** being filled with all unrighteousness, sexual immorality, wickedness, covetousness, maliciousness; full of envy, murder, strife, deceit, evil-mindedness; they are whisperers, **30** backbiters, haters of God, violent, proud, boasters, inventors of evil things, disobedient to parents, **31** undiscerning, untrustworthy, unloving, unforgiving, unmerciful; **32** who, knowing the righteous judgment of God, that those who practice such things are deserving of death, not only do the same but also approve of those who practice them."

1 Corinthians 10:1-11: "**1** Moreover, brethren, I do not want you to be unaware that all our fathers were under the cloud, all passed through the sea, **2** all were baptized into Moses in the cloud and in the sea, **3** all ate the same spiritual food, **4** and all drank the same spiritual drink. For they drank of that spiritual Rock that followed them, and that Rock was Christ. **5** But with most of them God was not well pleased, for their bodies were scattered in the wilderness **6** Now these things became our examples, to the intent that we should not lust after evil things as they also lusted. **7** And do not become idolaters as were some of them. As it is written, "The people sat down to eat and drink, and rose up to play." **8** Nor let us commit sexual immorality, as some of them did, and in one day twenty-three thousand fell; **9** nor let us tempt Christ, as some of them also tempted, and were destroyed by serpents; **10** nor complain, as some of them also complained, and were destroyed by the destroyer. **11** Now all these things happened to them as examples, and

they were written for our admonition, upon whom the ends of the ages have come."

Yes, these are long passages of scripture, and I could write another book just on the exposition of these scriptures. It might be worthwhile to read them again carefully. In these selected passages we could summarize by saying they all express inappropriate ways of dealing with sin. We have all sinned as Romans 3:23 tells us; none of us are perfect. It has been my experience in my own life as well as every single Christian I have ever known, that we are all guilty of committing sins on a regular basis. The denial of that fact is even a sin in itself; that of denial and/or pride.

The point of all of this is not so much to convince us that we are regularly committing sins in life, but to call close attention to how we deal with our sins. It saddens my heart as I have witnessed so many, and I emphasize "so many" believers who struggle with facing up to their sins and appropriately dealing them by confession, repentance, and restoration. The four main sub-points to this matter: justifying, minimizing, rationalizing, and blame-shifting is the "normal" responses of believers to their sins. Rather than being courageous enough to face our sins head on, we often find it easier to employ one or more of these four ways of seeking to escape the discomfort of the exposure of our sins.

It is painful to face your sins. It can be embarrassing, or even worse. The consequences of sin are never easy to face and should never be avoided. In fact, in Numbers 32:23, we are simply told that you can "be sure your sin will find you out." Eventually, this is true. No one really escapes the consequences of their sin, no matter how small or how deep it is buried!

I believe one of the most dangerous consequences of inappropriately dealing with our sins, is that we lose the fear of God! This happens in a way that we may not even realize it until it's too late. Considering our teaching in this book, this should be a "wake-up" call for each of us. Especially those of us who understand and desire the fear of God in our lives to be a strong part of our Christian life.

The scriptures above illustrate just how God feels and acts toward unresolved sins in our lives. In the Romans passage in particular it states, "for the wrath of God is revealed from heaven against ungodliness and unrighteousness of men." Seriously consider with me, "the wrath of God?" Who wants the wrath of God being poured out in their lives? Please don't think this is only for the worst of unrepentant sinners… this is for ALL unrepentant sinners which includes me and you! Our little "game" of justifying, minimizing, rationalizing, or blaming others for our thoughts and actions just falls so short and drains the fear of God right out of our lives.

May we hear the voice of the Lord and the conviction of the Holy Spirit that we may begin to seriously, honestly, and sincerely appropriately dealing with the sins in our life! Fear God!!!

6. Sexual Immorality

Consider these scriptures:

1 Corinthians 10:1-11: "__1__ Moreover, brethren, I do not want you to be unaware that all our fathers were under the cloud, all passed through the sea, __2__ all were baptized into Moses in the cloud and in the sea, __3__ all ate the same spiritual food, __4__ and all drank the same spiritual drink. For they drank of that spiritual Rock that followed them, and that Rock was Christ. __5__ But with most of them God was not well pleased, for their bodies were scattered in the wilderness __6__ Now these things became our examples, to the intent that we should not lust after evil things as they also lusted. __7__ And do not become idolaters as were some of them. As it is written, "The people sat down to eat and drink, and rose up to play." __8__ Nor let us commit sexual immorality, as some of them did, and in one day twenty-three thousand fell; __9__ nor let us tempt Christ, as some of them also tempted, and were destroyed by serpents; __10__ nor complain, as some of them also complained, and were destroyed by the destroyer. __11__ Now all these things happened to them as examples, and they were written for our admonition, upon whom the ends of the ages have come.

1 Thessalonians 4:1-8: "__1__ Finally then, brethren, we urge and exhort in the Lord Jesus that you should *abound more and more, just as you received from us how you ought to walk and to please God; **2** for you know what commandments we gave you through the Lord Jesus. **3** For this is the will of God, your sanctification: that you should abstain from sexual immorality; **4** that each of you should know how to possess his own vessel in sanctification and honor, **5** not in passion of lust, like the Gentiles who do not know God; **6** that no one should take advantage of and defraud his brother in this matter, because the Lord is the avenger of all such, as we also forewarned you and testified. **7** For God did not call us to uncleanness, but in holiness. **8** Therefore he who rejects this does not reject man, but God, who has also given us His Holy Spirit.*

*Proverbs 5:20-23: "**20** For why should you, my son, be enraptured by an immoral woman, And be embraced in the arms of a seductress? **21** For the ways of man are before the eyes of the Lord, And He ponders all his paths. **22** His own iniquities entrap the wicked man, And he is caught in the cords of his sin. **23** He shall die for lack of instruction, And in the greatness of his folly he shall go astray.*

Obviously, sexual immorality is a sin and is for sure covered clearly in previous points, but it does deserve some special attention. The sexual drive is quite strong in mankind and has led into so much perversion. We are living in a world culture that has turned so many things upside down and calling what was once wrong, right today. Especially when it comes to sexual matters, this has been a focus of attack by liberal thinking people seeking to rewrite what is good and healthy for children and adults.

Let us first define what is sexual immorality just in case anyone is confused from all the conversations today. Sexual immorality in general is any kind of sexual activity outside of the marriage of a man and a woman. Even in marriage when sexual activity takes on a form of degradation of one or both partners where it is unhealthy and destructive can be considered sexually immoral. Sex outside of marriage whether with other partners (adult or children), pornography, or even sex with animals is a part of sexual immorality.

Our listed scriptures are just a sample of what the Bible has to say about this subject. The listed verses clearly tell us how dangerous sexual immorality is and how God feels and responds to it in the lives of people. I Corinthians 10:8 tells us that because God's people were committing sexual immorality that in one day 23,000 people died. That is quite serious! In addition, in 1 Thessalonians 4:6, it says that God is an "avenger" to release judgment on those practicing sexual immorality.

It is not a challenging task to understand that sexual immorality can cause us to lose the fear of God. Again, because it is so prevalent among believers today, scripture holds a dire warning for us to consider, understand, and take personal action to abstain from it at all times. The times and pressures of today present a difficult barrier to walking in purity, but it is necessary in order to grow in the fear of God. Remember, every believer has the presence and power of the Holy Spirit living inside of them to assist along with remembering one of the features of the fear of God is ACCOUNTABILITY. God is with us all the time and sees what we are thinking and doing. We need to cease following the direction into sexual immorality and Fear God!!!

7. Idolatry

Consider these scriptures:

> *1 Corinthians 10:6-7:* "**6** *Now these things became our examples, to the intent that we should not lust after evil things as they also lusted.* **7** *And do not become idolaters as were some of them. As it is written, "The people sat down to eat and drink, and rose up to play."*

> *I Corinthians 6:14-22:* "**14** *Therefore, my beloved, flee from idolatry.* **15** *I speak as to wise men; judge for yourselves what I say.* **16** *The cup of blessing which we bless, is it not the communion of the blood of Christ? The bread which we break, is it not the communion of the body of Christ?* **17** *For we, though many, are one bread and one body; for we all partake of that one bread.* **18** *Observe Israel after the flesh: Are not*

*those who eat of the sacrifices partakers of the altar? **19** What am I saying then? That an idol is anything, or what is offered to idols is anything? **20** Rather, that the things which the Gentiles sacrifice they sacrifice to demons and not to God, and I do not want you to have fellowship with demons. **21** You cannot drink the cup of the Lord and the cup of demons; you cannot partake of the Lord's table and of the table of demons. **22** Or do we provoke the Lord to jealousy? Are we stronger than He?"*

1 Samuel 15:23: "For rebellion is as the sin of witchcraft, And stubbornness is as iniquity and idolatry. Because you have rejected the word of the Lord, He also has rejected you from being king."

Jonah 2:8: "Those who regard worthless idols Forsake their own Mercy."

Idolatry is seen in the Old Testament as one of the most dangerous sins of God's people. Over and over again we discover God's judgment falling on His people because of their idolatry. In the New Testament, really nothing has changed. Idolatry is still a terrible sin and has horrible consequences attached to it.

The rationale that seems to arise in the hearts of many Christians today is that they do not actually fall down and worship idols, as if we need a carved image of some god in our homes. So, idolatry is thought of as more a foreign concept that is not committed by the majority of Christians today. Oh no, what a huge mistake in thinking! Idolatry is making anything more valuable or more of a priority than God. This could be money or the pursuit of it. It can be possessions, sports, famous people or music groups, power, position, etc., etc. We could go on and on at this point, but we will not. I think you get the point. Anything that draws your time and attention away from God and glorifying Him is idolatry.

The fear of God is all about putting God first in your life and making Him your priority. Glorifying God is the direct result of fearing Him. One of the seven features of fearing God is being devoted to His word as I have mentioned many times. When our focus and devotion is on something else, we are committing idolatry. The whole matter of idolatry will cause you to lose the fear of God. Losing the fear of God leads down a path of idolatry. This is a vicious cycle that has many destructive consequences!

The scriptures above are only an example of many scriptures that speak to the same issue. These are enough to get our attention to what the Bible says about idolatry. And what is really scary is that idolatry is closely connected to demonic activity in our lives. It's not something we should take lightly as the Apostle Paul indicates in 1 Corinthians 6:14-22. Deepening your understanding of this matter of idolatry can go a long way in helping you to guard your hearts and maintain the fear of God!

8. Love for this present world

Consider these scriptures:

Hebrews 13:5: "Let your conduct be without covetousness; be content with such things as you have. For He Himself has said, "I will never leave you nor forsake you."

James 4:4: "Adulterers and adulteresses! Do you not know that friendship with the world is enmity with God? Whoever therefore wants to be a friend of the world makes himself an enemy of God."

1 John 2:15: "Do not love the world or the things in the world. If anyone loves the world, the love of the Father is not in him."

*2 Peter 3:3-4: "**3** knowing this first: that scoffers will come in the last days, walking according to their own lusts, **4** and saying, "Where is the promise of His coming? For since the fathers fell asleep, all things continue as they were from the beginning of creation."*

James 4:4 says it best. You just cannot love this world and maintain the fear of God in your life. If loving the world makes you an enemy of God, it is impossible to have the fear of God. Operating in the fear of God clearly and simply runs counter to loving this present world. Unfortunately, the design of commercials seems to purposely draw us away from the Lord creating a love for this world through deceptive temptation; or to get you to look to the world to get your needs met, or to obtain some higher level of satisfaction. Seriously, is there anything better than God Himself?

The clearer we can understand the importance of dying to ourselves every day and surrendering to the Lord the better off we will be. Loving this present world will slowly drain away the fear of God from our lives. May we take the scriptural admonitions to avoid this like a deadly plague, which it really is in disguise! May our time and efforts be focused on building the fear of God and loving Him only!

9. Disregarding the Word of God.

Consider these scriptures:

> *1 Samuel 15:20-23:* "**20** *And Saul said to Samuel, "But I have obeyed the voice of the Lord, and gone on the mission on which the Lord sent me, and brought back Agag king of Amalek; I have utterly destroyed the Amalekites.* **21** *But the people took of the plunder, sheep and oxen, the best of the things which should have been utterly destroyed, to sacrifice to the Lord your God in Gilgal."* **22** *So Samuel said: "Has the Lord as great delight in burnt offerings and sacrifices, As in obeying the voice of the Lord? Behold, to obey*

is better than sacrifice, And to heed than the fat of rams. **23** For rebellion is as the sin of witchcraft, And stubbornness is as iniquity and idolatry. Because you have rejected the word of the Lord, He also has rejected you from being king."

Psalm 112:1: "Praise the Lord! Blessed is the man who fears the Lord, Who delights greatly in His commandments."

Ecclesiastes 12:13: "Let us hear the conclusion of the whole matter: Fear God and keep His commandments, For this is man's all."

John 8:31-32: "**31** Then Jesus said to those Jews who believed Him, "If you abide in My word, you are My disciples indeed. **32** And you shall know the truth, and the truth shall make you free."

Mathew 4:4: "But He answered and said, "It is written, 'Man shall not live by bread alone, but by every word that proceeds from the mouth of God.' "

Romans 10:17: "So then faith comes by hearing, and hearing by the word of God."

Romans 15:4: "For whatever things were written before were written for our learning, that we through *the patience and comfort of the Scriptures might have hope."*

Deuteronomy 5:29: "Oh, that they had such a heart in them that they would fear Me and always keep all My commandments, that it might be well with them and with their children forever!

*Deuteronomy 6:2, 24: "**2** that you may fear the Lord your God, to keep all His statutes and His commandments which I command you, you and your son and your grandson, all the days of your life, and that your days may be prolonged."*

__24__ And the Lord commanded us to observe all these statutes, to fear the Lord our God, for our good always, that He might preserve us alive, as it is this day."

A feature of fearing God as previously stated is being devoted to the word of God, so it almost goes without saying that if you disregard the word of God then the result would be losing the fear of God. The scriptures listed above provide strong evidence of this fact. These verses emphasize the vital importance of having God's word as an intimate experience in our lives. It must be said that devotion to the word of God is a daily encounter and experience. In addition, this is a never-ending activity of our lives in Christ, and it never grows old or stale.

The three verses from Deuteronomy at the end of the list are there to show how the fear of God is so directly linked to being devoted to the word of God. Don't miss the emphasis of these verses.

In our busy lives with so many demands for our time, it may be easy to lose sight of the importance of being in the word of God. All my Christian life I have heard and preached about how important having a daily quiet time is, focusing on the scriptures. I have heard a million excuses of why people find it difficult to maintain a regular and meaningful time every day to be in the word. With all that we have discussed throughout this book, I can only hope that you have come to a deeper conviction regarding this matter. Just remember that disregarding the Word or putting it off for assorted reasons will only lead to the fear of God draining out of your heart and mind, ultimately losing the fear of God altogether, although you may maintain active membership and activities in your church. Yes, faithful Christians with little or no fear of God! I am afraid to say that this is the general picture of the church today. This reveals the reason for such little power and problematic lives within the ranks of churches. This is a warning to us all!

10. Fear of man, circumstances, devil, world, and death.

Consider these scriptures:

Proverbs 29:25: "The fear of man brings a snare, But whoever trusts in the Lord shall be safe."

1 Samuel 15:24: "Then Saul said to Samuel, "I have sinned, for I have transgressed the commandment of the Lord and your words, because I feared the people and obeyed their voice."

*Hebrews 2:14-15: "**14** Inasmuch then as the children have partaken of flesh and blood, He Himself likewise shared in the same, that through death He might destroy him who had the power of death, that is, the devil, **15** and release those who through fear of death were all their lifetime subject to bondage."*

As we consider this particular point, it is important to understand that this fear of man, circumstances, devil, world, and death is quite different from the fear of God. This "fear" is more about being afraid of these things to the point where you might become paralyzed and unable to move or accomplish some task. It also may result in making poor decisions or choices that would be contrary to God's word and will for your life. A third effect of this kind of "fear" is simply holding you back or making poor decisions.

From the above verses, we find this "fear" can lead you into bondage. In addition, it can be seen as a sin or possibly a lifestyle of sin. However you look at it, it can result in leading you away from the fear of God and obviously cause you to lose the fear of God in your life. You cannot have both. One pushes the other out of your life!

11. Unresolved hurt

Consider these scriptures:

*Genesis 4:1-15: "**1** Now Adam knew Eve his wife, and she conceived and bore Cain, and said, "I have acquired a man from the Lord." **2** Then she bore again, this time his brother Abel. Now Abel was a keeper of sheep, but Cain was a tiller of the ground. **3** And in the process of time it came to pass that Cain brought an offering of the fruit of the ground to the Lord. **4** Abel also brought of the firstborn of his flock and of their fat. And the Lord respected Abel and his offering, **5** but He did not respect Cain and his offering. And Cain was very angry, and his countenance fell. **6** So the Lord said to Cain, "Why are you angry? And why has your countenance fallen? **7** If you do well, will you not be accepted? And if you do not do well, sin lies at the door. And its desire is for you, but you should rule over it." **8** Now Cain talked with Abel his brother; and it came to pass, when they were in the* field, that Cain rose up against Abel his brother and killed him. **9** Then the Lord said to Cain, "Where is Abel your brother?" He said, "I do not know. Am I my brother's keeper?" **10** And He said, "What have you done? The voice of your brother's blood cries out to Me from the ground. **11** So now you are cursed from the earth, which has opened its mouth to receive your brother's blood from your hand. **12** When you till the ground, it shall no longer yield its strength to you. A fugitive and a vagabond you shall be on the earth." **13** And Cain said to the Lord, "My punishment is greater than I can bear! **14** Surely You have driven me out this day from the face of the ground; I shall be hidden from Your face; I shall be a fugitive and a vagabond on the earth, and it will happen that anyone who finds me will kill me." **15** And the Lord said to him, "Therefore, whoever kills Cain, vengeance shall be taken on him sevenfold." And the Lord set a mark on Cain, lest anyone finding him should kill him."

1 Samuel 18:6-9: "**6** Now it had happened as they were coming home, when David was returning from the slaughter of the Philistine, that the women had come out of all the cities of Israel, singing and dancing, to meet King Saul, with tambourines, with joy, and with musical instruments. **7** So the women sang as they danced, and said: "Saul has slain his thousands, And David his ten thousands." **8** Then Saul was very angry, and the saying displeased him; and

he said, "They have ascribed to David ten thousands, and to me they have ascribed only thousands. Now what more can he have but the kingdom?" **9** So Saul eyed David from that day forward."

Luke 23:32-43: "**32** There were also two others, criminals, led with Him to be put to death. **33** And when they had come to the place called Calvary, there they crucified Him, and the criminals, one on the right hand and the other on the left. **34** Then Jesus said, "Father, forgive them, for they do not know what they do." And they divided His garments and cast lots. **35** And the people stood looking on. But even the rulers with them sneered, saying, "He saved others; let Him save Himself if He is the Christ, the chosen of God." **36** The soldiers also mocked Him, coming and offering Him sour wine **37** and saying, "If You are the King of the Jews, save Yourself." **38** And an inscription also was written over Him in letters of Greek, Latin, and Hebrew: THIS IS THE KING OF THE JEWS **39** Then one of the criminals who were hanged blasphemed Him, saying, "If You are the Christ, save Yourself and us." **40** But the other, answering, rebuked him, saying, "Do you not even fear God, seeing you are under the same condemnation? **41** And we indeed justly, for we receive the due reward of our deeds; but this Man has done nothing wrong." **42** Then he said to Jesus, "Lord, remember me when You come into Your kingdom." **43** And Jesus *said to him, "Assuredly, I say to you, today you will be with Me in Paradise."*

Luke 4:18-19: "**18** *"The Spirit of the Lord is upon Me, Because He has anointed Me To preach the gospel to the poor; He has sent Me to heal the brokenhearted, To proclaim liberty to the captives And recovery of sight to the blind, To set at liberty those who are oppressed;* **19** *To proclaim the acceptable year of the Lord."*

These are a couple of long passages of scriptures to tell the stories of a few examples of unresolved hurt in people's lives and the results coming forth. There is so much to be said from each of these stories. My comments will be kept at a minimum to the best of my ability, keeping in mind the matter of losing the fear of God because of harboring unresolved hurt in our hearts.

There is no one on the face of the earth that can experience life for very long without experiencing emotional hurt of some kind. Some have serious trauma from multiple events and some a little less hurt, but everyone experiences pain and hurt at times in their lives. The big question is: what do we **do** with the hurts when they come? Too many people do a very poor job of managing their hurts in an appropriate way that truly leads to the healing of Christ flowing into their hearts. The result is the hurt and pain are submerged deep inside often being reflected as anger, anxiety, shame, and disassociation; disconnecting from meaningful and lasting relationships. The mental health field is overflowing with people in desperate need for Christ's healing rather than simply counseling to learn how to better function in life! Again, the terrible result is the draining away of the fear of God that we all so need in our Christian life.

In these stories from the scriptures, we first find Cain living a cursed life passed on to his children. Secondly, we see King Saul losing his relationship with God and others, becoming a man with a murderous spirit. Thirdly, we see a thief on a cross next to Jesus dying in his bitterness and pain rather than experiencing the loving forgiveness of Jesus and having an eternal future in heaven with Christ. The other thief actually points out the lack of the fear of God in his fellow thief as the cause of his horrible future being determined.

I have to take a moment to mention what I have found that is so powerful in the verses in Luke 4:18-19. In fact, after seven years of research and study leading to my PhD, I was able to formulate a way and means of leading Christians into a form of Christian Inner Healing based on these verses that have helped so many people experience healing and finally resolve their hurts and wounds. My Doctoral Dissertation was written based on those seven years of research, biblical exposition, and the development of a practical way to experience this important inner healing, resolving hurts!

Again, I must say that believers have become masters at hiding, pretending nothing is wrong, and basically covering up their hurts and wounds. I actually have heard some people say that holding on to their hurts has provided the motivation for building their character into who they are today. Now, it is true that God uses everything for our good, but don't be fooled into thinking that holding on to past hurts will be beneficial to you. The opposite is true. And I must say that when you are able to experience the supernatural, divine healing from Jesus, the freedom and power that comes is beyond awesome! As well as providing a wide avenue to travel on building the fear of God so much stronger in your life!

12. We simply do not choose the fear of God

Consider these verses:

> Proverbs 1:27-29: "**27** *When your terror comes like a storm, And your destruction comes like a whirlwind, When distress and anguish come upon you.* **28** *"Then they will call on me, but I will not answer; They will seek me diligently, but they will not find me.* **29** *Because they hated knowledge And did not choose the fear of the Lord,"*

This last reason why people lose the fear of God is quite a simple one. The verse in Proverbs just simply states that these people "did not choose the fear of the Lord;" we all have our own free will. Just because you are a Christian, which doesn't mean you can't exercise your free will for good or for evil. Yes, after gaining insight and understanding about the fear of God, you might just say, "that's not for me. That's too much and I really am not interested in having that kind of deep relationship with God. I just want God to be available when I need Him, in other words, I need Him to be my "puppet" to come rescue me in tough times. I don't need to have Him as Lord over my life, telling me what to do!"

What a warning is given to us in these verses in Proverbs! I need to quote them as an answer to the thoughts written above… "**27** *When your terror comes like a storm, And your destruction comes like a whirlwind, When distress and anguish come upon you.* **28** *"Then they will call on me, but I will not answer; They will seek me diligently, but they will not find me.* **29** *Because they hated knowledge And did not choose the fear of the Lord,"*

As a "watchman on the wall", I cry out to everyone reading this, "Fear God!" Make your priority in your Christian life one to spend quality time on a consistent basis, building the fear of God in your life!

Conclusion to This Chapter

There are so many causes that lead to losing the fear of God in your life. These twelve as listed and discussed really are only representative of the causes. There are more for sure and as you walk in this way, you will be able to identify others. These twelve causes can serve as warning signs for us along the way and hopefully will be used by the Holy Spirit to help guide us. Fearing God is so important and is a vital part of living out our Christian life. May you have an ever-burning desire to honestly evaluate yourself and to make whatever course corrections are in order for you to Fear God more than most!

CHAPTER SIX:

The Complete List of All the Verses in the Bible that Speak to the Fear of God

NOTE: There are many scriptural passages found in this book. Many of them are supportive to the particular point being made. These following verses are all **specifically** dealing with the **fear of God**. The point of having all of these here is to provide significant evidence that the fear of God is extremely important and must be given it's rightful place as a priority in the Christian life.

> **Gen 20:11** [11] And Abraham said, "Because I thought, surely the fear of God is not in this place; and they will kill me on account of my wife.

Gen 42:18 Then Joseph said to them the third day, "Do this and live, for I fear God:

Exo 9:30 ³⁰ But as for you and your servants, I know that you will not yet fear the LORD God.

Exo 18:21 ²¹ Moreover you shall select from all the people able men, such as fear God, men of truth, hating covetousness; and place such over them to be rulers of thousands, rulers of hundreds, rulers of fifties, and rulers of tens.

Lev 19:14 You shall not curse the deaf, nor put a stumbling block before the blind, but shall fear your God: I am the LORD.

Lev 19:32 You shall [a]rise before the gray headed and honor the presence of an old man, and fear your God: I am the LORD.

Lev 25:36 You shall [a]rise before the gray headed and honor the presence of an old man, and fear your God: I am the LORD.

Lev 25:43 You shall [a]rise before the gray headed and honor the presence of an old man, and fear your God: I am the LORD.

Deu 4:10 especially concerning the day you stood before the Lord your God in Horeb, when the Lord said to me, 'Gather the people to Me, and I will let them hear My words, that they may learn to fear Me all the days they live on the earth, and that they may teach their children.'

Deu 5:29 Oh, that they had such a heart in them that they would fear Me and always keep all My commandments, that it might be well with them and with their children forever!

Deu 6:2 that you may fear the Lord your God, to keep all His statutes and His commandments which I command you, you and your son and your grandson, all the days of your life, and that your days may be prolonged.

Deu 6:13 You shall fear the Lord your God and serve Him, and shall take oaths in His name.

Deu 6:24 And the Lord commanded us to [a] observe all these [b]statutes, to fear the Lord our God, for our good always, that He might preserve us alive, as it is [c]this day.

Deu 8:6 Therefore you shall keep the commandments of the Lord your God, to walk in His ways and to fear Him.

Deu 10:12 *And now, Israel, what does the* Lord *your God require of you, but to fear the* Lord *your God, to walk in all His ways and to love Him, to serve the* Lord *your God with all your heart and with all your soul,*

Deu 10:20 *You shall fear the* Lord *your God; you shall serve Him, and to Him you shall hold fast, and take oaths in His name.*

Deu 13:4 *You shall fear the* Lord *your God; you shall serve Him, and to Him you shall hold fast, and take oaths in His name.*

Deu 13:11 *So all Israel shall hear and fear, and not again do such wickedness as this among you.*

Deu 14:23 *And you shall eat before the* Lord *your God, in the place where He chooses to make His name abide, the tithe of your grain and your new wine and your oil, of the firstborn of your herds and your flocks, that you may learn to fear the* Lord *your God always.*

Deu 17:13 *And all the people shall hear and fear, and no longer act presumptuously. And all the people shall hear and fear, and no longer act presumptuously.*

Deu 17:19 And it shall be with him, and he shall read it all the days of his life, that he may learn to fear the LORD his God and be careful to observe all the words of this law and these statutes,

Deu 19:20 And those who remain shall hear and fear, and hereafter they shall not again commit such evil among you.

Deu 21:21 Then all the men of his city shall stone him to death with stones; so you shall put away the evil from among you, and all Israel shall hear and fear.

Deu 28:58 "If you do not carefully observe all the words of this law that are written in this book, that you may fear this glorious and awesome name, THE LORD YOUR GOD,

Deu 31:12 Gather the people together, men and women and little ones, and the stranger who is within your gates, that they may hear and that they may learn to fear the LORD your God and carefully observe all the words of this law,

Deu 31:13 and that their children, who have not known it, may hear and learn to fear the LORD your God as long as you live in the land which you cross the Jordan to possess."

Jos 4:24 *that all the peoples of the earth may know the hand of the* Lord, *that it is mighty, that you may fear the* Lord *your God* [a]*forever."*

Jos 22:25 *For the* Lord *has made the Jordan a border between you and us, you children of Reuben and children of Gad. You have no part in the* Lord." *So your descendants would make our descendants cease fearing the* Lord.'

Jos 24:14 *Now therefore, fear the* Lord, *serve Him in sincerity and in truth, and put away the gods which your fathers served on the other side of* [a]*the River and in Egypt. Serve the* Lord!

1 Sam 11:7 *o he took a yoke of oxen and cut them in pieces, and sent them throughout all the territory of Israel by the hands of messengers, saying, "Whoever does not go out with Saul and Samuel to battle, so it shall be done to his oxen."*

1 Sam 12:14 *If you fear the* Lord *and serve Him and obey His voice, and do not rebel against the commandment of the* Lord, *then both you and the king who reigns over you will continue following the* Lord *your God.*

1 Sam 12:24 *Only fear the* LORD*, and serve Him in truth with all your heart; for consider what great things He has done for you.*

2 Sam 23:3 *The God of Israel said,*
The Rock of Israel spoke to me:
'He who rules over men must be just,
Ruling in the fear of God.

1 King 8:40 *that they may fear You all the days that they live in the land which You gave to our fathers.*

1 King 8:43 *hear in heaven Your dwelling place, and do according to all for which the foreigner calls to You, that all peoples of the earth may know Your name and fear You, as do Your people Israel, and that they may know that this temple which I have built is called by Your name.*

1 King 18:12 *And it shall come to pass, as soon as I am gone from you, that the Spirit of the* LORD *will carry you to a place I do not know; so when I go and tell Ahab, and he cannot find you, he will kill me. But I your servant have feared the* LORD *from my youth.*

2 King 4:1 *A certain woman of the wives of the sons of the prophets cried out to Elisha, saying, "Your servant my husband is dead, and you know that* your servant feared the Lord. And the creditor is coming to take my two sons to be his slaves."

2King 17:28 Then one of the priests whom they had carried away from Samaria came and dwelt in Bethel, and taught them how they should fear the Lord.

2 King 17:34 To this day they continue practicing the former rituals; they do not fear the Lord, nor do they follow their statutes or their ordinances, or the law and commandment which the Lord had commanded the children of Jacob, whom He named Israel,

2King 17:39 But the Lord your God you shall fear; and He will deliver you from the hand of all your enemies."

1 Chr 16:30 Tremble before Him, all the earth. The world also is firmly established,
It shall not be moved.

2 Chr 6:33 then hear from heaven Your dwelling place, and do according to all for which the foreigner calls to You, that all peoples of the earth may know Your name and fear You, as do Your people Israel, and that they may know that [a]this temple which I have built is called by Your name.

2 Chr 14:14 *Then they defeated all the cities around Gerar, for the fear of the Lord came upon them; and they plundered all the cities, for there was exceedingly much [a]spoil in them.*

2 Chr 17:9-10 *⁹ So they taught in Judah, and had the Book of the Law of the Lord with them; they went throughout all the cities of Judah and taught the people. ¹⁰ And the fear of the Lord fell on all the kingdoms of the lands that were around Judah, so that they did not make war against Jehoshaphat.*

2 Chr 19:5-7 *⁵ Then he set judges in the land throughout all the fortified cities of Judah, city by city, ⁶ and said to the judges, "Take heed to what you are doing, for you do not judge for man but for the Lord, who is with you [a]in the judgment. ⁷ Now therefore, let the fear of the Lord be upon you; take care and do it, for there is no iniquity with the Lord our God, no partiality, nor taking of bribes."*

2 Chr 19:9 *And he commanded them, saying, "Thus you shall act in the fear of the Lord, faithfully and with a loyal heart*

2 Chr 20:29 *And the fear of God was on all the kingdoms of those countries when they heard that the LORD had fought against the enemies of Israel.*

Neh 5:9 *Then I said, "What you are doing is not good. Should you not walk in the fear of our God because of the reproach of the nations, our enemies?*

Neh 5:15 *But the former governors who were before me laid burdens on the people, and took from them bread and wine, besides forty shekels of silver. Yes, even their servants bore rule over the people, but I did not do so, because of the fear of God.*

Neh 1:11 *O Lord, I pray, please let Your ear be attentive to the prayer of Your servant, and to the prayer of Your servants who desire to fear Your name; and let Your servant prosper this day, I pray, and grant him mercy in the sight of this man."*

Job 1:9 *So Satan answered the LORD and said, "Does Job fear God for nothing?*

Jon 6:14 *"To him who is [a]afflicted, kindness should be shown by his friend,
Even though he forsakes the fear of the Almighty.*

Job 9:34-35 ³⁴ *Let Him take His rod away from me,*
And do not let dread of Him terrify me.
³⁵ *Then I would speak and not fear Him,*
But it is not so with me.

Job 15:1-4 *Then Eliphaz the Temanite answered and said:* ² *"Should a wise man answer with empty knowledge, And fill [a]himself with the east wind?* ³ *Should he reason with unprofitable talk, Or by speeches with which he can do no good?* ⁴ *Yes, you cast off fear, And restrain [b]prayer before God.*

Job 28:28 *And to man He said,*
'Behold, the fear of the Lord, that is wisdom,
And to depart from evil is understanding.'"

Job 37:24 *Therefore men fear Him;*
He shows no partiality to any who are wise of heart."

Psa 2:11 *Serve the* L*ord* *with fear,*
And rejoice with trembling.

Psa 5:7 *But as for me, I will come into Your house in the multitude of Your mercy;*
In fear of You I will worship toward [a]Your holy temple.

Psa 15:4 *In whose eyes a vile person is despised,*
But he honors those who fear the Lord;
He who swears to his own hurt and does not change;

Psa 19:9 *The fear of the* Lord *is clean,*
enduring forever;
The judgments of the Lord *are true and righteous*
altogether.

Psa 22:23 *You who fear the* Lord, *praise Him!*
All you [a]descendants of Jacob, glorify Him,
And fear Him, all you offspring of Israel!

Psa 25:14 *The secret of the* Lord *is with those who fear Him,*
And He will show them His covenant.

Psa 31:19 *Oh, how great is Your goodness,*
Which You have laid up for those who fear You,
Which You have prepared for those who trust in You
In the presence of the sons of men!

Psa 33:8 *Let all the earth fear the* Lord;
Let all the inhabitants of the world stand in awe
of Him.

Psa 33:18 *Behold, the eye of the* Lord *is on those who fear Him,*
On those who hope in His mercy,

Psa 34:7 The [a]angel of the Lord encamps all
around those who fear Him,
And delivers them.

Psa 34:9 Oh, fear the Lord, you His saints!
There is no [a]want to those who fear Him.

Psa 34:11 Come, you children, listen to me;
I will teach you the fear of the Lord.

Psa 36:11 Let not the foot of pride come against me,
And let not the hand of the wicked drive me away.

Psa 36:1 An oracle within my heart concerning the
transgression of the wicked:
There is no fear of God before his eyes.

Psa 40:3 He has put a new song in my mouth—
Praise to our God;
Many will see it and fear,
And will trust in the Lord.

Psa 52:5-7 ⁵ God shall likewise destroy you forever;
He shall take you away, and pluck you out
of your dwelling place,
And uproot you from the land of the living. Selah
⁶ The righteous also shall see and fear,
And shall laugh at him, saying,

⁷ *"Here is the man who did not make God his strength,*
But trusted in the abundance of his riches,
And strengthened himself in his [a]wickedness."

Psa 53:5 *There they are in great fear*
Where no fear was,
For God has scattered the bones of him who encamps against you;
You have put them to shame,
Because God has despised them.

Psa 55:19 *God will hear, and afflict them,*
Even He who abides from of old. Selah
Because they do not change,
Therefore they do not fear God.

Psa 61:5 *For You, O God, have heard my vows;*
You have given me the heritage of those who fear Your name.

Psa 64:9 *All men shall fear,*
And shall declare the work of God;
For they shall wisely consider His doing.

Psa 66:16 *Come and hear, all you who fear God,*
And I will declare what He has done for my soul.

Psa 67:7 *God shall bless us,*
And all the ends of the earth shall fear Him.

Psa 72:5 *They shall fear You*
As long as the sun and moon endure,
Throughout all generations.

Psa 85:9 *Surely His salvation is near to those who fear Him,*
That glory may dwell in our land.

Psa 86:11 *Teach me Your way, O LORD;*
I will walk in Your truth;
[a]Unite my heart to fear Your name.

Psa 90:11 *Who knows the power of Your anger?*
For as the fear of You, so is Your wrath.

Psa 96:9 *Oh, worship the LORD in the beauty of holiness!*
Tremble before Him, all the earth.

Psa 102:15 *So the [a]nations shall fear the name of the LORD,*
And all the kings of the earth Your glory.

Psa 103:11 *For as the heavens are high above the earth,*
So great is His mercy toward those who fear Him;

Psa 103:13 As a father pities his children,
So the Lord pities those who fear Him.

Psa 103:17 But the mercy of the Lord is from everlasting to everlasting
On those who fear Him,
And His righteousness to children's children,

Psa 111:5 He has given food to those who fear Him;
He will ever be mindful of His covenant.

Psa 111:10 The fear of the Lord is the beginning of wisdom;
A good understanding have all those who do His commandments.
His praise endures forever.

Psa 115:11 You who fear the Lord,
trust in the Lord;
He is their help and their shield.

Psa 115:13 He will bless those who fear the Lord,
Both small and great.

Psa 118: 4 Let those who fear the Lord now say,
"His mercy endures forever."

Psa 119:38 Establish Your word to Your servant,
Who is devoted to fearing You.

Psa 119:63 *I am a companion of all who fear You,*
And of those who keep Your precepts.

Psa 119:74 *Those who fear You will be glad when they see me,*
Because I have hoped in Your word.

Psa 119:79 *Let those who fear You turn to me,*
Those who know Your testimonies.

Psa 119:120 *My flesh trembles for fear of You,*
And I am afraid of Your judgments.

Psa 135:20 *Bless the Lord. O house of Levi!*
You who fear the Lord, bless the Lord!

Psa 145: 19 *He will fulfill the desire of those who fear Him;*
He also will hear their cry and save them.

Psa 147:11 *The* L*ord* *takes pleasure in those who fear Him,*
In those who hope in His mercy.

Prov 1:7 *The fear of the* L*ord* *is the beginning of knowledge,*
But fools despise wisdom and instruction.

Prov 2:5 *Then you will understand the fear of the* L*ord*,
And find the knowledge of God.

Prov 3:7 *Do not be wise in your own eyes;*
Fear the L*ord and depart from evil.*

Prov 8:13 *The fear of the* L*ord is to hate evil;*
Pride and arrogance and the evil way
And the perverse mouth I hate.

Prov 9:10 *"The fear of the* L*ord is the beginning of wisdom,*
And the knowledge of the Holy One
is understanding.

Prov 10:27 *The fear of the* L*ord prolongs days,*
But the years of the wicked will be shortened.

Prov 14:26 *In the fear of the* L*ord there is strong confidence,*
And His children will have a place of refuge.

Prov 14:27 *The fear of the* L*ord is a fountain of life,*
To turn one away from the snares of death.

Prov 15:16 *Better is a little with the fear of the* L*ord*,
Than great treasure with trouble.

Prov 15:33 *The fear of the* Lord *is the instruction of wisdom,*
And before honor is humility.

Prov 16:6 *In mercy and truth*
Atonement is provided for iniquity;
And by the fear of the Lord *one departs from evil.*

Prov 19:23 *The fear of the* Lord *leads to life,*
And he who has it will abide in satisfaction;
He will not be visited with evil.

Prov 22:4 *By humility and the fear of the* Lord
Are riches and honor and life.

Prov 23:17 *Do not let your heart envy sinners,*
But be zealous for the fear of the Lord *all the day;*

Prov 24:21 *My son, fear the* Lord *and the king;*
Do not associate with those given to change;

Ecc 3:14 *I know that whatever God does,*
It shall be forever.
Nothing can be added to it,
And nothing taken from it.
God does it, that men should fear before Him.

Ecc 5:7 *For in the multitude of dreams and many words there is also vanity. But fear God.*

Ecc 8:12 Though a sinner does evil a hundred times, and his days are prolonged, yet I surely know that it will be well with those who fear God, who fear before Him.

Ecc 12:13 Let us hear the conclusion
of the whole matter:
Fear God and keep His commandments,
For this is man's all.

Isa 2:10 Enter into the rock, and hide in the dust,
From the terror of the Lord
And the glory of His majesty.

Isa 2:19 They shall go into the holes of the rocks,
And into the caves of the [a]earth,
From the terror of the Lord
And the glory of His majesty,
When He arises to shake the earth mightily.

Isa 2:21 To go into the clefts of the rocks,
And into the crags of the rugged rocks,
From the terror of the Lord
And the glory of His majesty,
When He arises to shake the earth mightily.

Isa 8:13 The Lord of hosts, Him you shall hallow;
Let Him be your fear,
And let Him be your dread.

Isa 11:2 *The Spirit of the* Lord *shall rest upon Him,*
The Spirit of wisdom and understanding,
The Spirit of counsel and might,
The Spirit of knowledge and of the fear of the Lord.

Isa 11:3 *His delight is in the fear of the* Lord,
And He shall not judge by the sight of His eyes,
Nor decide by the hearing of His ears;
<u>Read full chapter</u>

Isa 25:3 *Therefore the strong people will glorify You;*
The city of the [a]*terrible nations will fear You.*

Isa 29:13 *Therefore the Lord said:*
"Inasmuch as these people draw near with their mouths
And honor Me with their lips,
But have removed their hearts far from Me,
And their fear toward Me is taught by the commandment of men,

Isa 29:23 *But when he sees his children, The work of My hands, in his midst,*
They will hallow My name, And hallow the Holy One of Jacob,
And fear the God of Israel.

Isa 33:6 *Wisdom and knowledge will be the stability of your times,*

And the strength of salvation;
The fear of the LORD is His treasure.

Isa 59:19
So shall they fear
The name of the LORD from the west,
And His glory from the rising of the sun;
When the enemy comes in like a flood,
The Spirit of the LORD will lift up a standard against him.

Isa 63:17
O LORD, why have You made us stray from Your ways,
And hardened our heart from Your fear?
Return for Your servants' sake,
The tribes of Your inheritance.

Jer 2:19 "Therefore I will yet [a]bring charges against you," says the LORD,
"And against your children's children I will bring charges.

Jer 5:24
They do not say in their heart,
"Let us now fear the LORD our God,
Who gives rain, both the former and the latter, in its season.

*He reserves for us the appointed weeks
of the harvest."*

Jer 5:22
*Do you not fear Me?' says the Lord.
'Will you not tremble at My presence,
Who have placed the sand as the bound of the sea,
By a perpetual decree, that it cannot pass beyond it?
And though its waves toss to and fro,
Yet they cannot prevail;
Though they roar, yet they cannot pass over it.*

Jer 26:19 *Did Hezekiah king of Judah and all Judah ever put him to death? Did he not fear the Lord and seek the Lord's favor? And the Lord relented concerning the doom which He had pronounced against them. But we are doing great evil against ourselves."*

Jer 32:39 *then I will give them one heart and one way, that they may fear Me forever, for the good of them and their children after them.*

Jer 32:40 *And I will make an everlasting covenant with them, that I will not turn away from doing them good; but I will put My fear in their hearts so that they will not depart from Me.*

Jer 33:9 *Then it shall be to Me a name of joy, a praise, and an honor before all nations of the earth, who shall hear all the good that I do to them; they shall fear and tremble for all the goodness and all the prosperity that I provide for it.'*

Dan 6:26 *I make a decree that in every dominion of my kingdom men must tremble and fear before the God of Daniel.*

Hos 3:5 *Afterward the children of Israel shall return and seek the Lord their God and David their king. They shall fear the Lord and His goodness in the latter days.*

Amo 3:8
A lion has roared!
Who will not fear?
The Lord God has spoken!
Who can but prophesy?

Jon 1:9 *So he said to them, "I am a Hebrew; and I fear [a]the Lord, the God of heaven, who made the sea and the dry land."*

Mic 7:17
They shall lick the dust like a serpent;
They shall crawl from their holes like [a]snakes of the earth.

They shall be afraid of the LORD our God,
And shall fear because of You.

Hag 1:12 Then Zerubbabel the son of Shealtiel, and Joshua the son of Jehozadak, the high priest, with all the remnant of the people, obeyed the voice of the LORD their God, and the words of Haggai the prophet, as the LORD their God had sent him; and the people feared the presence of the LORD.

Mal 1:6
"A son honors his father,
And a servant his master.
If then I am the Father,
Where is My honor?
And if I am a Master,
Where is My reverence?
Says the LORD of hosts
To you priests who despise My name.
Yet you say, 'In what way have we despised Your name?'

Mal 2:5
"My covenant was with him, one of life and peace,
And I gave them to him that he might fear Me;
So he feared Me
And was reverent before My name.

Mal 3:5
And I will come near you for judgment;
I will be a swift witness
Against sorcerers,
Against adulterers,
Against perjurers,
Against those who exploit wage earners and widows and orphans,
And against those who turn away an alien—
Because they do not fear Me,"
Says the L*ord* *of hosts.*

Mal 4:2
But to you who fear My name
The Sun of Righteousness shall arise
With healing in His wings;
And you shall go out
And grow fat like stall-fed calves.

Mt 10:28 And do not fear those who kill the body but cannot kill the soul. But rather fear Him who is able to destroy both soul and body in [a]hell.

Lk 5:26 And they were all amazed, and they glorified God and were filled with fear, saying, "We have seen strange things today!"

Lk 7:16 Then fear [a] came upon all, and they glorified God, saying, "A great prophet has risen up among us"; and, "God has visited His people."

Lk 12:5 But I will show you whom you should fear: Fear Him who, after He has killed, has power to cast into hell; yes, I say to you, fear Him!

Lk 18:4 And he would not for a while; but afterward he said within himself, 'Though I do not fear God nor regard man,

Lk 23:40 But the other, answering, rebuked him, saying, "Do you not even fear God, seeing you are under the same condemnation?

Act 2:43 Then fear came upon every soul, and many wonders and signs were done through the apostles.

Act 5:5 Then Ananias, hearing these words, fell down and breathed his last. So great fear came upon all those who heard these things.

Act 5:11 So great fear came upon all the church and upon all who heard these things.

Act 9:31 Then the churches throughout all Judea, Galilee, and Samaria had peace and were edified.

[b] *And walking in the fear of the Lord and in the comfort of the Holy Spirit, they were multiplied.*

Act 13:16 *Then Paul stood up, and motioning with his hand said, "Men of Israel, and you who fear God, listen:*

Act 19:17 *This became known both to all Jews and Greeks dwelling in Ephesus; and fear fell on them all, and the name of the Lord Jesus was magnified.*

Rom 3:18 *"There is no fear of God before their eyes."*

1 Cor 2:3 *I was with you in weakness, in fear, and in much trembling.*

2 Cor 7:1 *Therefore, having these promises, beloved, let us cleanse ourselves from all filthiness of the flesh and spirit, perfecting holiness in the fear of God.*

2 Cor 7:15 *And his affections are greater for you as he remembers the obedience of you all, how with fear and trembling you received him.*

Eph 5:21 *submitting to one another in the fear of God.*

Eph 6:5 *Bondservants, be obedient to those who are your masters according to the flesh, with fear and trembling, in sincerity of heart, as to Christ;*

Phil 2:12 *Therefore, my beloved, as you have always obeyed, not as in my presence only, but now much more in my absence, work out your own salvation with fear and trembling;*

Col 3:22 *Bondservants, obey in all things your masters according to the flesh, not with eyeservice, as men-pleasers, but in sincerity of heart, fearing God.*

1 Tim 5:20 *Those who are sinning rebuke in the presence of all, that the rest also may fear.*

Heb 4:1 *Therefore, since a promise remains of entering His rest, let us fear lest any of you seem to have come short of it.*

Heb 11:7 *By faith Noah, being divinely warned of things not yet seen, moved with godly fear, prepared an ark for the saving of his household, by which he condemned the world and became heir of the righteousness which is according to faith.*

Heb 12:28 *Therefore, since we are receiving a kingdom which cannot be shaken, let us have grace,* by which we [a]may serve God acceptably with reverence and godly fear.

1 Pet 1:17 And if you call on the Father, who without partiality judges according to each one's work, conduct yourselves throughout the time of your [a] stay here in fear;

1 Pet 2:17 Honor all people. Love the brotherhood. Fear God. Honor the king.

1 Pet 3:2 when they observe your chaste conduct accompanied by fear.

1 Pet 3:15 But [a]sanctify the Lord God in your hearts, and always be ready to give a defense to everyone who asks you a reason for the hope that is in you, with meekness and fear;

Rev 11:18
The nations were angry, and
Your [a]wrath has come,
And the time of the dead, that they
should be judged,
And that You should reward Your servants the prophets and the saints,
And those who fear Your name, small and great,
And should destroy those who destroy the earth."

Rev 14:7 *saying with a loud voice, "Fear God and give glory to Him, for the hour of His judgment has come; and worship Him who made heaven and earth, the sea and springs of water."*

Rev 15:4
*Who shall not fear You, O Lord, and
glorify Your name?
For You alone are holy.
For all nations shall come and worship before You,
For Your judgments have been manifested."*

Rev 19:5
Then a voice came from the throne, saying, "Praise our God, all you His servants and those who fear Him, both[a] small and great!"

CHAPTER SEVEN:

The Fear of God Assessment Tool and Evaluation

NOTE: Seriously consider each one and being completely honest with yourself rate yourself on each one from a 0 to 10. 0 means none at all and a 10 means you do this perfectly.

1. **Awareness:** <u>An awareness of God's awesome continual presence around us and in us.</u>
I am a _____ (0-10)

2. **Awe:** <u>A deep sense of awe, wonder, and respect of who God is and what He does.</u>

I am a _____ (0-10)

3. Submission: *Genuine connection and submission to Jesus as Lord as well as Savior of our life*
I am a _____ (0-10)

4. Honor: *A commitment to honor, respect, glorify, and magnify Jesus in all that we do and think.*
I am a _____ (0-10)

5. Accountability: *An understanding and living out a lifestyle of our personal accountability to Him of our thoughts, motives, actions, and words.*
I am a _____ (0-10)

6. Word-Filled: *A serious commitment to be devoted to His word.*
I am a _____ (0-10)

7. Humility: *A commitment to walk in humility and be constantly crucifying our pride.*
I am a _____ (0-10)

Evaluation

0-20 = Little or no fear of God at all

21-35 = Some fear of God

36-52 = Average fear of God

53-70 = More fear of God than most

This can be an eye-opening experience as well as a clear indicator on where you need to put some serious work with the Holy Spirit helping you… "Working out your own salvation in fear and trembling."

Conclusion

THIS BOOK WILL NOT BE the most popular Christian book ever written. In fact, it may be one of those books we might never want to read again.

Several of the prophets in the Old Testament were told by God that they would experience persecution for bringing His word to the people. And God told a couple of them that hardly anyone would listen but would even reject what they were given by God. I am not sure what the reception will be of this word, but what I do have is a serious conviction that this book and message is from God!

I believe this is a strong prophetic word to the entire Christian Church around the world. This defines and explains the missing ingredient that is the source of most of all Christian's problems today. Understanding and applying these truths in our lives will result in a world of believers making themselves ready for the coming of the Lord!

Taking the seven features of what the fear of God is and making them the focus of our work and activity is the most important part of this book. Obviously, this is not an easy task, nor will it be short-term. It will involve changes in our lifestyle, our time schedule, and our lifetime, but it will be worth it!

What you have read is the conclusion of three years of devoted study and teaching and a full and comprehensive search through the entire Bible to know everything we need to understand about the fear of God. As the subtitle of this book asks, "Are you afraid yet? You should be!" is the beginning of discovering and embracing a life where the fear of God is up front and central to our Christian lives!

May the Lord help us to no longer live without the fear of God!

I leave you with the three passages from the Bible that we began with. God bless you and lead you to **FEAR GOD** all the days of your life!...

1. Ecclesiastes 12:13-14 *"Let us hear the conclusion of the whole matter: Fear God and keep His commandments, for this is man's all. For God will bring every work into judgment, including every secret thing, whether good or evil."*

2. Philippians 2:12-13 *"Therefore my beloved, as you have always obeyed, not as in my presence only,* *but now much more in my absence, work out your own salvation with fear and trembling; for it is God who works in you both to will and to do for His good pleasure."*

3. Matthew 10:28 *"And do not fear those who kill the body but cannot kill the soul. But rather fear Him who is able to destroy both soul and body in hell."*

About the Author

DR. EVANS has uniquely blended the two disciplines of spirituality and psychology in both training and practice. He holds a B.Min. from Florida Baptist College in Graceville, Florida and a M.Div. from Southwestern Baptist Theological Seminary in Fort Worth, Texas, pastoring churches in Florida and Texas since 1978. Dr. Evans is the founder of the Grace Christian Fellowship movement and is the founder and Chairman of Grace Christian Worldwide Ministries. Both he and his wife Mandy do mission work in East Central Africa and the southern part of the Philippines providing leadership and supervision to over 400 hundred Grace Christian Fellowship Churches.

Also, Dr. Evans is a licensed Christian Marriage and Family Therapist and a Certified Pastoral Addictions Counselor in the State of Florida. He holds a Ph.D. in the field of psychology with the Commonwealth Open University in the British Virgin Islands. Dr. Evans was the Director of Outreach Services for the Community Behavioral Health Center in Brevard County, Florida for 28 years. He and his family continue to be active in their local church as well as preaching, teaching, and counseling in many venues. You can contact him easily at Drevans0825@gmail.com

WA

www.ingramcontent.com/pod-product-compliance
Lightning Source LLC
Chambersburg PA
CBHW060130190426
43200CB00039B/2678